The Arts and Crafts Sourcebook

Charlotte Kelley

The Arts and Crafts Sourcebook

Thames & Hudson

First published in the United Kingdom in 2001
by Thames & Hudson Ltd, 181A High Holborn,
London WC1V 7QX

British Library Cataloguing-in-Publication Data
A catalogue record for this book is available
from the British Library

ISBN 0-500-28295-1

Printed and bound in China

QUAR.STF

CONTENTS

INTRODUCTION

Arts and Crafts style is as compelling and relevant today as it was in its heyday in the mid-nineteenth and early twentieth centuries. Much more than just a style of decoration, the Arts and Crafts Movement began as one of social reform, and the Arts and Crafts style echoes the Movement's founding principles of integrity and social responsibility. With its hallmark simple designs, beautiful materials, and honest craftsmanship, it is no wonder that the look remains an enduring cornerstone of modern interior design to this day.

No single style is entirely representative of the Movement, which may be one reason for its enduring popularity. The Arts and Crafts look suits a broad range of tastes and homes, while the styles mingle well with more modern design elements. The Japanese lines of Frank Lloyd Wright or Charles Rennie Mackintosh sit perfectly with a minimalist urban decor, while William Morris's floral textiles and cottage furniture bring softness and warmth to a family home. Similarly, in the USA the Mission and Prairie styles associated with Gustav Stickley and Greene & Greene are as at home in a country ranch as they are in a city loft.

The roots of the Arts and Crafts Movement lie in the aesthetic approach to interior design and interest in social reform that originated with the reformers and writers A. W. N. Pugin and John Ruskin. Changes brought about by the Industrial Revolution in mid-Victorian Britain inspired a quest for a return to simplicity, honesty and beauty. As people flooded from the countryside into cities to work in newly built factories, they left behind traditions of home and family life. Followers of the Movement believed that the factory system stripped workers of their dignity, and that a return to true craftsmanship and its artisan way of life was paramount to a healthy society. Designers like William Morris, C. F. A. Voysey and Charles Rennie Mackintosh founded a whole new

'The great advantage and charm of the Morrisian method is that it lends itself to either simplicity or splendour. You might be almost as plain as Thoreau, with a rush-bottomed chair, piece of matting and oaken trestle table; or you might have gold and lustre (the choice ware of William de Morgan) gleaming from the sideboard, and jewelled light in the windows, and walls hung with arras tapestry.'
Walter Crane

Gustav Stickley's American Craftsman style of furniture and lighting is beautifully complemented by the neutral walls, wooden flooring and Indian drugget rug.

design ethos that rejected the overly ornate decorations and machine-made furniture, textiles and ornaments of the Victorian era. Morris revived traditional weaving, dyeing and textile printing – crafts that had already succumbed to the lure of industrialisation – and William de Morgan's handmade lustre-glazed ceramics with Persian, mediaeval and floral motifs were works of art in themselves.

Once these designs were brought to the United States by style ambassadors such as playwright Oscar Wilde and retail giant Arthur Lasenby Liberty, American designers and craftsmen took the ideas to a new level. In the second half of the nineteenth century, America was experiencing its own industrial boom, giving rise to a new moneyed middle class. Designers like Gustav Stickley, Greene & Greene and architect-designer Frank Lloyd Wright developed the Arts and Crafts style, drawing inspiration from the Shaker Movement and the crafts of the indigenous American people. And unlike the British Arts and Crafts Movement, American designers embraced the machine, which enabled more people to buy Arts and Crafts pieces – real design and quality for the masses.

Affluent British and American families commissioned architects to build the most impressive houses affordable, and these were built with local wood and stone to blend into the surrounding landscape. Rooms were open and spacious, enabling family and friends to gather together in comfort. Dust-gatherers such as knick-knacks and heavy curtains were discouraged, and fresh air was recommended for good health. Sleeping porches and cushioned window seats were built to allow access to light and scenery. The natural theme spread to walls and floors: polished wood panelling was chosen,

> 'Have nothing in your houses that you do not know to be useful or believe to be beautiful.'
> **William Morris**

William Morris's original design for Avon chintz, c.1886.

Frank Lloyd Wright's geometric style of furniture, lighting and stained glass dominates the interior of the Meyer May house in Michigan (USA), which he completed in 1909.

teamed with wallpaper featuring floral motifs. Light muslin, linen and cotton curtains with stylised repeats brought a touch of nature into the home, and beautifully crafted furniture revealed the grain of the local wood.

Today's Arts and Crafts interior begins with simple wooden flooring softened with sisal, jute, rush or coir matting for hard-wearing areas, and oriental, Persian or Native American rugs for more colourful accents. Walls panelled up to the dado rail or shoulder height warm up or lighten the room, depending on whether the wood is left natural and polished, or painted white. Above the panelling, walls may be painted white or a natural shade, or covered in wallpaper with repeating floral motifs. Windows simply decorated with lightweight curtains – muslin, cotton or linen panels hung from wooden poles – add another layer of texture to the primarily neutral walls.

Tiffany-style standard lamp with popular bamboo stained-glass motif and brass base.

This simple canvas allows furniture to stand out as a feature in its own right. The beauty of the wood grain and the excellent craftsmanship make Arts and Crafts furniture truly wonderful to behold – if not entirely comfortable to sit on. Fabric-covered or leather-upholstered cushions soften hard wooden seats. Authentic Arts and Crafts upholstery fabrics are widely available today through key suppliers such as Sanderson and Liberty, and cushions fashioned from these classic patterns will add authenticity to a room.

Lamps have always been a hallmark of Arts

Oak Arts and Crafts dining table and chairs suit this airy octagonal room in an English house designed by C. F. A. Voysey.

and Crafts decoration and numerous modern designers have adapted or reproduced the Craftsman, Mackintosh and Tiffany styles. A standard lamp in a corner and a strategically placed table lamp add pools of light to a room and can highlight favourite ornaments. Unlike Victorian rooms, which were awash with knick-knacks, the Arts and Crafts ideal was to use only objects that were deemed to be both beautiful and necessary.

The Movement borrowed extensively from other cultures and periods, owing debts to India, Japan, the Middle East, Scandinavia, Celtic Ireland, Byzantium, as well as mediaeval Europe and Renaissance Italy (for example, Indian carpets, Japanese design, Scandinavian colours, Celtic and mediaeval motifs). Today, the ease of international travel makes it ever more possible to bring home ornaments, rugs and cushions that resonate with the Arts and Crafts aesthetic.

Although the Arts and Crafts Movement waned in popularity after the First World War, the 1980s saw a revival in the Movement's craftsmanship and materials. Collectors began to snap up originals such as Voysey and Stickley furniture or Tiffany lamps, and these days most original pieces are rare and expensive. However, there are still enough 'finds' on the market to make the hunt for treasure exciting and worthwhile.

This book is intended as an introduction to Arts and Crafts styles, and pinpoints the main designs and

'The root of all reform lies in the individual and [that] the life of the individual is shaped mainly by home surroundings.'
Gustav Stickley

First issue of *The Craftsman* published by Gustav Stickley in October 1901.

Stickley settle upholstered in burgundy leather, still available today from the Stickley workshop in New York State.

themes of the Movement. Some readers will be keen to collect originals, but for those unable to buy original pieces, suppliers will produce Arts and Crafts-inspired pieces or reproductions on commission.

'There are many designers today who have taken the Arts and Crafts style as an inspiration or starting point.'

In fact, there are those who see the current revival more as an evolution of the Arts and Crafts style. There are many designers today who have taken the style as an inspiration or starting point, and have created beautiful and lasting pieces. These articles of furniture, fabrics, rugs and ornaments are much easier to find. Reproduction furniture is available from suppliers such as Stickley or Greene & Greene, and original designs of wallpaper and carpets are still in production today through companies such as Sanderson and Burrows.

Reproduction William de Morgan tile designs are available from specialist suppliers such as Kenneth Clark Ceramics.

There is no doubt that the Arts and Crafts Movement succeeded on a design level, although given that its products remained largely the province of the middle-class home, the Movement's socialist ethic was not entirely fulfilled. Thanks to the availability of quality goods and higher standards of living today, we now have the opportunity to redress this balance.

William Morris's wallpaper designs are still in production by companies such as Sanderson's.

William Morris's Tulip and Rose pattern is now available as a tapestry cushion from Designer's Forum.

HOW TO USE THIS BOOK

Each feature spread shows original and modern Arts and Crafts-style rooms, with a remarkable variety of colours, patterns, ornaments and styles of furniture. The other spreads in the book concentrate on the details common to the Movement.

Feature spread A full-colour, inspirational photograph of an Arts and Crafts-style room, with captions explaining the different elements in the picture.

Other spreads Details of floor coverings, textiles, furniture and ornaments featured in an Arts and Crafts home, plus a photograph of similar objects *in situ*.

INTRODUCTION TO THE TYPE OF ROOM FEATURED IN THE SPREAD.

ARTS AND CRAFTS FURNITURE, ORNAMENTS AND STYLING.

ANNOTATED PICTURE OF THE ROOM SET SHOWING THE LOCATION OF THE CAPTIONED OBJECTS.

CAPTIONS EXPLAINING THE DIFFERENT ELEMENTS IN THE ROOM SET FEATURED.

CAPTIONED PHOTOGRAPHS OF ORIGINAL AND REPRODUCTION FURNITURE, TEXTILES AND ORNAMENTS.

BACKGROUND INFORMATION ON THE HISTORY AND DESIGNERS OF THE OBJECTS FEATURED ON THE PAGE.

ANNOTATED ILLUSTRATIONS SHOWING COMMON STYLES OF FURNITURE AND ORNAMENTS.

SAMPLES OF ORIGINAL AND REPRODUCTION TEXTILES, PAINTS, FLOORINGS, WALLPAPERS, ORNAMENTS, FURNITURE AND STAINED GLASS WINDOWS.

SMALL ORIGINAL AND MODERN ROOM SETS SHOWING THE FEATURED OBJECT *IN SITU*.

Chapter 1

WALLS AND FLOORS

Walls and floors are a backdrop for the furniture, textiles, and ornaments displayed in the home. The basic components of Arts and Crafts style include wooden floors, rugs, tiles, panelling and wallpaper.

BEDROOM
Arts and Crafts bedrooms, unlike Victorian bedchambers, were decorated in a **simple** and **light** style to provide a **peaceful haven** for sleep and, if necessary, convalescence or periods of **rest**. Free-standing furniture was encouraged, so that rooms were easier to keep clean and dust-free. Heavy velvet curtains and bedlinens were replaced with **muslins** and light chintzes, and dark decorations gave way to **plain walls** and light wallpapers. Bedcovers were often plain, **embroidered**, or were pretty, hand-made **patchwork quilts**.

The colour green was popular, as it complemented white walls and textiles with floral designs.

Oak wardrobe with heart-shaped Ruskin enamels, stylised lily fruitwood panels and cruciform ring handles. Although Arts and Crafts designers invented built-in wardrobes, free-standing furniture was encouraged to make thorough cleaning and dusting possible. **SEE PAGE 94**

A Liberty's rush-seated beech side chair fits neatly in the corner of the room. **SEE PAGE 64**

An oak bedside cabinet is the perfect place to put a table lamp and flowers or books. **SEE PAGE 94**

Pine chests are useful for storing bedlinens, quilts and blankets – especially in summer. They also provide an extra surface for books and accessories. **SEE PAGE 98**

Brass beds can be bought from furniture suppliers, or originals can often be sourced from antique markets. Painted or wooden beds are also an option. **SEE PAGE 94**

Plain, white walls and ceiling are the perfect backdrop to an Arts and Crafts bedroom. The green-painted beams add a colourful accent. **SEE PAGE 18**

Mackintosh-style cushions are still available from specialist suppliers and the Glasgow School of Art in Scotland. **SEE PAGE 52**

A patchwork quilt adds a cosy feel to a bedroom, and the fact that it is hand-crafted fits in well with the Arts and Crafts ideal. **SEE PAGE 52**

PAINT

White distempered **walls** were a feature of William Morris's rural retreats and were also popular with American Arts and Crafts designers. Should you opt for plain **white** walls you will need to find a pure shade. **Distemper** has a unique formula which can offer a very appealing chalky finish. Colour paints are a means of generating a particular atmosphere in a room.

The perfect Arts and Crafts canvas uses colours derived from nature.

Ideally, **colour** tones should be based on **natural** hues such as fresh green, serene blue, warm russet or classic cream.

CHOOSING PAINTS

White painted walls provide a neutral backdrop to an Arts and Crafts interior, but colour in a room can add warmth or atmosphere. Natural tones are best adhered to.

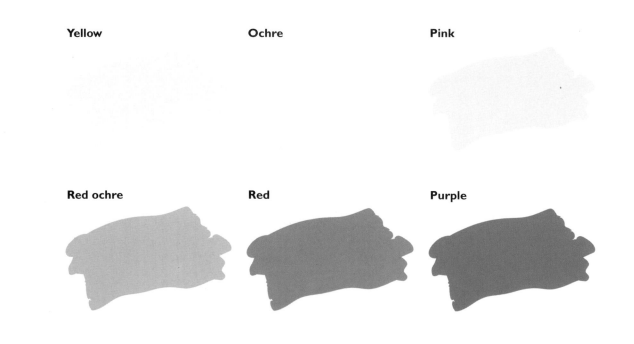

White

Chalk white

Yellow

Ochre

Pink

Red ochre

Red

Purple

A fine example of a carefully chosen wall finish, which is in complete harmony with the upholstery, the simple wooden floorboards and the Sussex bench. Morris advised painting woodwork white which, as you can see here, adds an additional element of freshness and light to the scheme.

Red-brown

Brown

Beige

Dark green

Light green

Green-blue

Soft blue

Mid blue

Dark blue

LIVING ROOM

Arts and Crafts designers would have hated the modern practice of matching every item of fabric and wallpaper in an interior. They thought nothing of **mixing** different **patterns** in a living room, as long as these were **selected** and **balanced** carefully to avoid visual confusion. This approach is evident in Morris's London home where a number of **different patterns** are juxtaposed in a **harmonious** manner. Morris's Willow wallpaper design and Chrysanthemum fabric for the curtains are **complemented** by Delft tiles, Oriental rugs and decorative furniture covers.

Floral patterned wallpaper – such as Willow Bough and Morris's small-flower creations – were a popular choice for living rooms and bedrooms.

Evenlode fabric, 1883. This was one of the first fabrics to be printed at Merton Abbey using the indigo discharge method.
SEE PAGE 46

Decorative tiles designed by Arts and Crafts ceramicist, William de Morgan.
SEE PAGE 38

Sussex armchair. One of the most popular furniture designs produced by Morris & Co., it works well in both an informal and formal interior.
SEE PAGE 64

Brer Rabbit fabric design. Philip Webb contributed the bird motifs in this design.
SEE PAGE 46

Willow wallpaper, perhaps the most popular of Morris's designs, inspired by a walk by his stream with his daughter.
SEE PAGE 22

William Morris and Jane Burden portraits. As this was Morris's London living room, there are a number of portraits of Morris and his wife, Jane.

Dutch Delft tiles. Morris had a deep affection for these folk designs in distinctive blue on a white tin-glazed background.
SEE PAGE 38

WALLPAPERS

Arts and Crafts wallpapers are characterised by **stylised** decorative forms inspired by **nature**. Through the use of continuous flowing lines and carefully organised **repeats**, William **Morris** was able to convey the spontaneous growth of nature in his wallpaper designs, producing over 40 of them during his illustrious career. This success had a notable influence on other **followers** of the Arts and Crafts Movement: C. F. A. **Voysey** and Walter Crane in England, the Wiener Werkstätte in Austria and

Wallpaper design by the Silver Studio, c.1890. The Silver Studio, founded by Arthur Silver, was responsible for some of Liberty's most popular and characteristic wallpaper designs, especially the famous Peacock Feather.

CHOOSING WALLPAPER

Wallpaper is only part of the decorative scheme and must be chosen in the context of the decor and proportions of the room in question. A horizontal pattern adds a touch of stability to large walls whereas a vertical pattern adds a sense of gravitas and formality to low wallls.

William Morris's Willow wallpaper, 1874. Willow still remains one of the most popular of Morris's wallpaper designs. It can be particularly effective in a bedroom or a bathroom thanks to its tranquil and fresh nature.

William Morris's Pomegranate or Fruit print is the most sophisticated of Morris's early wallpaper designs. He employed the branches of a fruit tree to articulate the repeat patterns of the design.

William Morris's Daisy. The first wallpaper design to be issued by Morris & Co. in 1862. The pattern is composed of alternate repeating plant motifs.

William Morris's small white and pink floral design. Morris's love of gardening and careful observation of British hedgerows is particularly evident in this modest yet beautifully constructed design.

William Morris's Trellis design, 1864. Although this was Morris's first wallpaper pattern, it was the third design issued. It is said to have been inspired by the rose trellis that ran along the garden at the Red House.

Fruit wallpaper designed by Morris and now supplied by Sanderson's. An early customer of Morris & Co., who decorated his living room with this design, observed proudly to a visitor that the flora on the walls of the room in which they sat seemed 'as if it was all a-growing'.

William Morris's Acanthus Leaves, wild rose on crimson background. Morris was particularly fond of the curving leaves of the acanthus, which he used over and over again, both as a main and subsidiary motif.

William Morris's powdered wallpaper, 1874. An uncharacteristically naïve design. Morris later abstracted the background pattern for his famous Willow designs.

York wallpaper, 1885. A fresh, tranquil pattern that reveals a fusion of the style of Morris's and Voysey's wallpaper designs.

William Morris's Trellis design, 1864. This wallpaper design is available in different colourways (see left). It is thought that the birds were the work of Morris's colleague, Philip Webb.

William Morris's Tulip design, 1875. Although this seems to be a simple design, it uses many different colours, and 18 wooden blocks were required to complete the pattern.

C. F. A. Voysey's 'Let Us Prey' design shows his characteristic simplicity of line. He often uses a bird motif, as in this print featuring a cat and bird repeat.

American designers such as Candace Wheeler. **Wallpapers** from the great Arts and Crafts designers are still **available** as machine- or hand-prints (the more expensive option). They can be used as a **continuous wall covering**, or above a dado rail or even on a single wall. It's important to ensure that the overall effect of a wallpaper design is in **harmony** with your furniture and other decorations. The design should be in accordance with the room's **proportions**; the larger the room the greater the size of repeats and the bolder the patterns possible. A smaller room should not be overwhelmed by its wallpaper. If you are

Silver Studio's Tulips print attributed to J. I. Kay, c.1898. Designs such as this one were sold by Silver Studio to leading manufacturers and stores in the UK, the USA and the Continent.

Burrows & Co.'s Chrysanthemum print. A simple and more tranquil interpretation of Morris's original design. The lacy leaves and flowing flowers reveal a Japanese influence.

Burrows & Co.'s Persis wall print in pale gold – a companion design to Persis Frieze. The main eucalyptus motif is a particularly good background against which to hang art.

Walter Crane's Francesca design. British-born designer Crane was one of the most effective promoters of the Arts and Crafts style in America, as well as a highly successful illustrator of children's books.

Burrows & Co.'s Lily and Rose. A fluid Scottish design with tendrils of lilies climbing in a diagonal line through conventionalised rose blossoms.

Burrows & Co.'s Gingko Leaf. A Japanese wallpaper design first published in New York in 1895. Japanese designs and motifs were popular with Arts and Crafts designers because of their linear simplicity and colour tones.

H. & H. Birge & Sons' highly textured wallpaper with embossed silver is designed along the lines of the Art Nouveau style on the Continent. Although the nature of this design would perhaps prove too elaborate for an entire wall area, it could be integrated with paler walls to provide a strong decorative focus.

Morris's Honeysuckle wallpaper design provides a fitting backdrop to a tiled fireplace featuring an oak mantel clock, c.1900, and a collection of metalware jugs and candlesticks.

Burrows & Co.'s Summer Street Damask print, attributed to John Dando Sedding. This subtle design of figs and fig leaves reveals a stylistic integration of the Arts and Crafts and Art Nouveau styles.

Sanderson's Jasmine print. The loose and meandering structure of this design provides a naturalistic effect, in that there is a distinct impression of organic and spontaneous growth.

Sanderson's Jasmine print. Many of Morris's wallpaper designs work well in a number of different colour combinations. The crossing of darker pink tones with lighter ones from behind creates a sense of depth.

Burrows & Co.'s Depden design. This design would be particularly effective as a dado, or as a band or ornament – wherever a simple repeating design is required.

Sanderson's Compton print is available in different colourways. The strong pattern would suit a tall hallway or staircase where the eye naturally looks upward.

Sanderson's Compton print. Although this pattern was originally designed by Morris for use as a fabric, it works equally well as wallpaper.

decorating your own home and wish to gain some idea of how different patterns will work together, it is often useful to assemble **samples** of wallpaper before committing yourself on a larger scale. **Explore** a number of different **colourways** and make sure that you view the samples by both natural and artificial **light**. Designers sometimes used a **frieze** above the panelling and below the ceiling line. The inspiration for the use of the **decorative** friezes came from the painted or stencilled borders that were favoured in mediaeval and Renaissance houses.

Swan Frieze by Voysey, the bird and animal designer par excellence of the nineteenth century. These swans, although highly naturalistic, are depicted in a simple, flat, stylised form, which is not too 'dishonestly' three-dimensional as was the case with many earlier Victorian frieze designs.

Sanderson's Fruit print is built up from the repetition of four rectangular elements. For such an early design, it appears relatively complex thanks to the strong diagonal element of the branches and leaves.

Sanderson's Willow Bough print. Morris's daughter May recorded that this popular design was inspired by a walk by their stream, when Morris pointed out to her the detail and variety in the leaf forms.

Sanderson's Honeysuckle print. May, a talented designer in her own right, favoured this design as it was the 'most mysterious and poetic – the very symbol of a garden tangle'.

Sanderson's Arbutus print. As its name implies, this is a highly verdant design and would help to achieve a formal, yet very fresh effect within a dining or sitting room.

Sanderson's Vine print. A bold design with soft, easy lines based on the naturally trailing branches of the vine plant. As there is plenty of movement in this pattern, it is equally suitable for a large or small wall.

Sanderson's Savernake print. A lighter and less elaborate interpretation of Morris's original, highly coloured Snakeshead design.

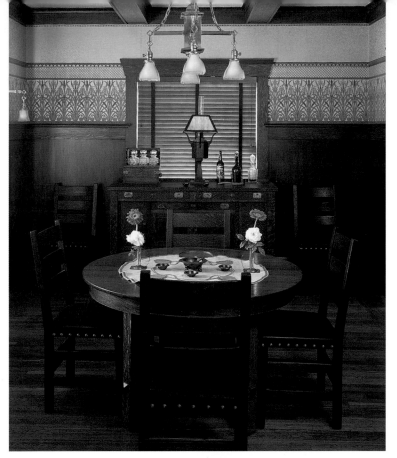

Iris Frieze by Bradbury and Bradbury provides a perfect cut-off point between the lower oak panelling and the wooden-beamed ceiling in this American dining room.

Burrows & Co.'s Persis Wall. An anonymous English design representative of the early Arts and Crafts movement. The dancing sprays of eucalyptus leaves would provide a decorative focus within a room or hallway broken up by many windows and doors.

Burrows & Co.'s Chauncy Frieze. A simple meandering design based on natural foliage motifs which works particularly well if applied in conjunction with plain whitewashed walls and in a room with exposed woodwork. Like the Persis Frieze, this design is available in a number of colourways.

DINING ROOM

Morris and his associates were keen supporters of wooden panelling. They believed it to be a wall surface which formed 'a **faultless background**, composed, **dignified** and **reposeful** as the heart could wish', and although it does not have the suggestiveness and variety of colour that tapestry possesses, it has 'a **poetry** of its own, a grave and **quiet** charm which is the essence of decorative content'. Wooden panelling worked well in dining rooms – an important room for the **family**, as this is where everyone gathered at least once a day.

Panels made of wood native to the locality are ideal for the walls of a room.

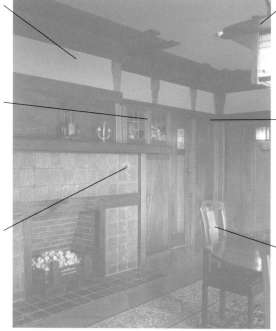

The white-beamed border adds a lighter touch to the heavily panelled oak walls.
SEE PAGE 18

These beautiful built-in display cabinets provide a decorative focus within the vast expanse of oak panelling.
SEE PAGE 86

Inlaid mother-of-pearl gives an Art Nouveau feel to the brick-coloured hearth tiles.
SEE PAGE 38

Wooden lighting accessories were a development particular to the Arts and Crafts movement in America.
SEE PAGE 120

The wooden-panelled walls evoke a log-cabin feel, traditional to American Craftsman architecture and interior design.
SEE PAGE 30

Signs of craftsmanship, such as the metal bolts of the chair, were left exposed with pride by Arts and Crafts designers.
SEE PAGE 64

PANELLING

Wooden panelling or **wainscoting** was a common feature of housing until the end of the eighteenth century and came into its own as a natural interior **feature** with the American Arts and Crafts Movement. Designers celebrated the **natural** and honest tones of wood or painted it **white** to add a touch of light to an interior. The type of **wood** varied according to the location of the house and the inclination of the architect or householder. **Oak** and native redwood were favoured by Frank Lloyd Wright and the Greene brothers for interior **beams** and panelling.

Different woods suit different rooms. Panels may also be painted or stained.

PANELS FOR YOUR ROOM

A wooden panelling scheme should use a wood that is natural in tone and that suits the proportions of the room. Oak panels are expensive, but cheaper woods such as pine or deal can be stained green or painted white. A veneer can even be used instead.

English oak

Fumed oak

Southern yellow pine

American red oak

American white ash

Maple

Elm

American walnut

Oak panelling creates a warm surround for the stunning tiled fireplace in Debenham House, London, designed by Halsey Ricardo.

The painted panelling acts as a perfect cut-off point between the ornate Honeysuckle wallpaper and the vivid, upholstered sofa.

STENCILS

Stencilling is a **print-making** technique that allows a design to be repeated on almost any surface. **Wall** and **furniture** stencilling was particularly popular in America and Europe during the nineteenth century before the mass production of wallpaper, especially as part of the overall decor of **bedrooms**. There is a wide range of pre-cut **stencils** on the market today and the technique itself is relatively **quick and easy** to master.

Pre-cut stencils can be used to create an individual look.

USING STENCILS

Stencil designs are an economic and versatile form of decoration. Carefully executed stencilling can offer an almost identical effect to more expensive runs of printed paper.

Roses

Flowers and leaves

Ivy

Stag

Peacock

Heart and leaves

Leafy branch

Tree

Willow and flower

Bamboo

Lettered stencilling adds a unique touch to the area between the decorative ceiling and the plain white walls of this bedroom in Holland House, London.

Leaves

Sun

Tulip group

Daisy girl

Flower

Rose

Pot and plant

Orchard

Trellis

HALLWAY

Gamble House in California – one of the finest examples of Prairie-style architecture, created by **Greene & Greene** – has impressed countless designers and architects since it was built in 1909. The **wood-lined walls** and **wooden flooring** give the hallway a feeling of airy space, and the large **oriental rugs** and **stained-glass** front doors add colour and **warmth**. The hall is the first room that most visitors see, and this is as **impressive** today as it must have been in its heyday.

Sisal matting is an attractive alternative to wooden floors, where more warmth underfoot may be desirable, especially in rooms like the bedroom. Sisal and rush should not be used in the bathroom or kitchen, as they don't react well to water.

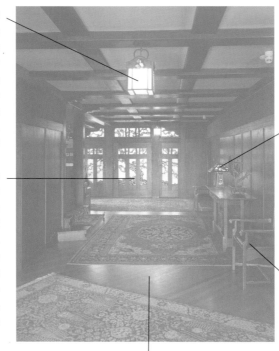

A Japanese influence figures heavily in Gamble House's architecture and interior decoration. The ceiling light in the hallway is similar to a Japanese lantern.
SEE PAGE 120

The art glass front door by Emil Lange features a jewel-like Tree-of-Life design inspired by Californian oak trees. The whole room glows when the sun shines through the glass in the mornings.
SEE PAGE 118

A Craftsman-style table lamp with stained-glass pattern sheds a pool of light on the wooden panelling and hall table, where visitors would have left their calling cards.
SEE PAGE 120

Greene & Greene chairs, upholstered in leather, provide a welcome seating area for visitors.
SEE PAGE 64

Wooden floors – despite their innate beauty – are often softened by boldly designed and highly coloured rugs. Make sure they are laid securely.
SEE PAGE 36

FLOORING

Plain polished **floorboards** complement an Arts and Crafts interior, and **woven** or **rush** rugs soften the look. Morris & Co.'s original woven rugs are now collectors' items, but modern versions of the designs are available. Gustav Stickley produced a range of **zigzag** rugs which proved hugely popular, but **floral** or geometric designs were also common. Modern **alternatives** are kelims and dhurries from India and the Middle East, Native American Indian Navaho rugs and knotted rugs.

Morris reproduction rug by Designer's Forum. Although Morris moved his loom from Hammersmith to the Merton Abbey works in 1881, his hand-knotted rugs, made with naturally dyed wools, were always known as Hammersmith carpets.

CHOICES FOR FLOORING

Older floorboards are rare and highly sought after, but hardwood and softwood laminates provide an affordable alternative. Sisal and rush matting, and rugs work well to soften the boards.

Natural wooden floor

Whitewashed wooden floor

Sisal matting

Polished wooden floor

Stained wooden floor

Rush matting

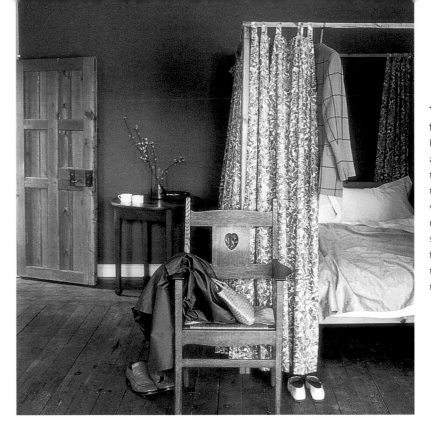

The wooden floorboards shown here not only provide an appropriate rustic feel to the room, but also offset the dark olive-green walls, which would otherwise be rather oppressive. The stripped pine door and furniture also complement the natural atmosphere of the room.

Native American Indian rug from Santa Fe, New Mexico (USA). Tribal rugs look magnificent on polished wooden floors and are even more popular today than during the Arts and Crafts era.

Voysey designed this rug in 1902 for Liberty and it was made in Donegal. Voysey's textile designs evolved from the use of traditional repeats based on historic forms to the simple flowering forms of this rug.

TILES

Arts and Crafts designers made it acceptable to cover a large **wall** area with tiles as part of a **decorative** scheme. William de Morgan, an associate of Morris, produced **art tiles** that were available on both sides of the Atlantic and proved especially suitable for **fireplace** surrounds. Art tiles were highly **popular in America**, where at least 50 tile companies were founded between 1875 and 1920.

Wlliam de Morgan Persian Moffat patterned tile produced at the ceramic works, Merton Abbey. Floral designs were rarely used on tiles until William de Morgan revived an interest in Islamic-inspired floral designs in the 1870s.

AUTHENTIC DESIGNS

Tiles by William de Morgan can be identified by a bold use of lustre glaze — usually with a copper or silver film — and strong designs inspired by natural and decorative motifs.

William de Morgan Animals frequently appeared in de Morgan's tiles, like this porcupine in red lustre on pottery.

William de Morgan This buff earthenware tile depicts a dragon, reflecting the interest in mediaeval tales at the time.

William de Morgan This earthenware tile with lustre glaze was decorated with dark blue, bird-like dragons.

William de Morgan A Persian-style flower adorns this tile most likely produced at his workshop in Chelsea.

William de Morgan An abstract floral pattern in blue and brown decorates this earthenware tile by de Morgan.

Halsey Ricardo worked closely with William de Morgan to produce the exotic colour scheme of this tiled hallway. The marble skirtings and pillar, combined with the jewel-like quality of the indigo tiles, give this hallway an Islamic feel.

Artichoke design tiles adorn the base of the fireplace in the Green Room at Kelmscott Manor, Morris's rural retreat in Gloucestershire.

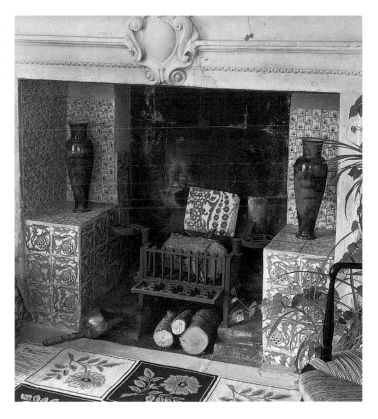

William de Morgan tiled frieze from Leighton House, London, which houses the famous Arab Hall. Oriental accents in decoration were common in the second half of the nineteenth century.

Today, **hand-painted** tiles in the Arts and Crafts style can be purchased at a relatively reasonable cost. Tiled walls are a highly **practical choice** for kitchens and bathrooms, and the odd pictorial design can offset any of the blandness a plain run of tiles could offer. **Flora** and **fauna** motifs are still popular choices – and **blue** is the dominant colour.

A few plain tiles in a complementary colour can relieve an otherwise overwhelming wall of patterned tiles. Here, a thistle design sits alongside a plain Engobe tile.

MODERN TILES

The Arts and Crafts look is popular for tiles, and some suppliers are especially thorough in their research into the correct designs and glazes to use. Flora and fauna predominate, and the patterned tiles are attractive as a fireplace surround or a splash-back above a kitchen or bedroom sink.

Nine Square Bough William Morris was keen on blue on white for domestic interiors and glazed plain white tiles with enamel.

Fruit Tree Morris's wallpaper designs were often used for other purposes, such as on glazed tiles.

Fish William de Morgan's fish design can be used singly, with plain Engobe tiles, as above right, or as a frieze.

Findon Daisy Designed by Morris, this tile looks especially good in a fireplace or above a sink in a bedroom.

Magpie Philip Webb originally designed this bird, which is now being reproduced by a modern supplier.

The Gothic revival assisted the rediscovery of geometric tile designs, which are still highly popular today. They are particularly practical for large tiled spaces such as floors and bathroom walls and can be beautifully complemented by pictorial tiles such as these Ironbridge tiles. The Encaustic Tile Company at Ironbridge remains in production today.

A sympathetically designed reproduction fireplace with Morris-style tiles can be the focal point of your living room, dining room, or even your bedroom or bathroom. There are many styles of tile that would suit this type of fireplace.

Chapter 2

TEXTILES
Arts and Crafts textiles suit many interior schemes and are still extremely popular. The king of Arts and Crafts textile design, William Morris, combined natural fabrics, hand-crafting techniques and stylised designs to produce timeless patterns that had a huge impact on curtains, wall hangings and upholstery of the day.

LIVING ROOM
Although William Morris never attempted to imitate nature, it was certainly one of his chief desires to **incorporate nature** into the domestic interior. In this living room, the **natural form** of his curtain fabric – Bird and Anemone – is enhanced by the **pale green** wall paint, **white floorboards** and the **simple** arrangement of **furniture**. Overall, there is a verdant and organic quality which bridges the gap between the **interior** and **exterior world**, which would prove particularly **soothing** in an urban environment.

Textile designs like Bird and Anemone are available in different colours, such as red (above) and green (main picture).

Bird and Anemone curtain fabric, a variation on Morris's original, famous Bird design.
SEE PAGE 46

A simple, yet elegant sofa upholstered in plain blue to complement the blue tones of the curtain fabric.
SEE PAGE 72

These cushion covers are subtly coordinated with the curtains without giving the scheme too uniform a look.
SEE PAGE 52

Pale greens, blues and creams were favoured colours for the walls in an Arts and Crafts interior.
SEE PAGE 18

The popularity of Morris's Sussex chairs has made them an essential component of an Arts and Crafts interior. Although they are now collectors' items, the basic style and design is still in demand as reproduction furniture.
SEE PAGE 64

White painted floorboards give a fresh quality and provide a neutral backdrop to the overall decorative scheme.
SEE PAGE 36

The pale and simply decorated rug softens the plain white floorboards.
SEE PAGE 36

CURTAINS

Fabric when **folded** and **draped** has a life of its own and Morris's **flowing motifs** based on natural forms suit a **simple** window treatment. Dense brocade patterns such as Iris and Larkspur add a sense of **urban grandeur** to a room, whereas designs such as Honeysuckle or Willow suit the **informality** of a rural cottage. Although the full range of Morris curtain-fabric designs is no longer available, Sanderson's has the right to print his designs and stocks about 20 patterns. Many commercial outlets can supply the later fabric **designs** of Candace Wheeler, Voysey and Walter Crane.

William Morris's Peacock and Dragon design, c.1878, shows off his revival of old techniques, including the use of vegetable dyes and block printing methods.

ARTS AND CRAFTS MATERIAL

Since the nineteenth century – largely as a result of the work of Arts and Crafts designers – cotton chintzes have been regarded as important artworks in their own right rather than as a mere backdrop to the rest of the interior decor.

Morris & Co.'s Jasmine Trail or Jasmine Trellis design. Morris frequently used the trellis motif as a means of structuring the repeats of a design.

Pair of Morris & Co. printed velveteen curtains by J. H. Dearle, c.1890. J. H. Dearle started out in life as Morris's assistant, but became responsible for a considerable amount of the firm's later design work.

Sanderson's Daisy print. Originally a wallpaper design, Daisy works well as a cotton fabric and is particularly suitable for a quiet bedroom or a country sitting room.

Sanderson's Fruit print. One of the main reasons for the success of Morris's chintzes was his use of natural dyes as opposed to the lurid and cheap aniline dyes common in the nineteenth century.

Sanderson's Chrysanthemum print. This simple structure of inter-twining stems is brought to life by Morris's passion for natural forms and understanding of how they grow.

Arts and Crafts cotton prints are equally at home in a modern interior as they are in more historical ones. From the second half of the nineteenth century onward, printed cottons replaced the use of heavy velveteens or woven fabrics for curtains. Morris, in particular, loved to explore the textual qualities of cloth and designed numerous patterns using natural fibres and dyes.

Morris & Co.'s Marigold design. Produced by Morris & Co. as a chintz and a wallpaper. Thanks to its neutral colour tones, this design is particularly suitable for bathroom or bedroom curtains in conjunction with plain white walls and woodwork.

Sanderson's Bird and Anemone print. Morris produced this design alongside Brer Rabbit and Strawberry Thief. All three designs reveal his romanticised vision of the English countryside.

Sanderson's Bird and Anemone print. As with many of Morris's wallpaper designs, curtain fabrics work effectively in different colour combinations.

Sanderson's Willow Bough print. Simple and fresh, this is one of Morris's curtain designs that can be used in conjunction with the same wallpaper pattern, without creating too heavy an effect.

Sanderson's Compton print. The rich claret, olive and light-brown colour tones of this fabric provide a particularly warm atmosphere to a room when used as a curtain fabric.

Sanderson's Honeysuckle print. A complex design in which the delicate, circular honeysuckle blossoms complement the more dominant stylised blooms.

WINDOW TREATMENTS
The best way to **display** a Morris or Arts and Crafts fabric of your own is to suspend it on **wooden rings** threaded along a polished wooden or metal **pole**. Elaborate fringes and trimmings should be avoided and the fabric should suit the decorative scheme of the room. By the end of the nineteenth century, window treatments were very **simple**, with American Arts and Crafts designers advocating the use of **white linen**, cotton or **translucent** net. **Plain cotton** curtains contrast well with internal pattern work such as wall hangings and brightly coloured rugs.

Candace Wheeler's 'Consider the lilies of the field' curtain. An embroidered and painted portière (door curtain) created by the American fabric and wallpaper designer Candace Wheeler in 1897.

HOW TO RECOGNISE ARTS AND CRAFTS WINDOW TREATMENTS

Metal pole and curtain rings

▶ BRASS FLORAL WALL SUPPORT

▶ METAL CURTAIN RINGS

Styling of curtains depends on the size and shape of the window, and the function of the room.

Wood panel

▼ WOOD PANEL CONCEALS CURTAIN HOOKS

Tie-top

▼ METAL CURTAIN POLE

▼ TIE-TOP

Pencil pleats

▼ PELMET HEADED PENCIL PLEATS

Wooden rail and metal rings

▼ COPPER CURTAIN RINGS

▼ WOODEN CURTAIN RAIL

Burrows & Co.'s Meadow Lily. This curtain works well in any style of home where a simple and lighter lace pattern is required. It is particularly suitable for a bathroom or kitchen, or anywhere where a little privacy is desired.

Burrows & Co.'s The Stag, designed by Voysey. The design is displayed to its best advantage when the curtain is hung full out.

Burrows & Co.'s Kelvin Rose panels. This panel features the famous Glasgow rose which was so integral to the work of Charles Rennie Mackintosh and the Glasgow School. Due to the relatively small scale of the design, it is best applied to a small bathroom or kitchen window.

Burrows & Co.'s Albertine panels. A Scottish design discovered by John Burrows in an English textile archive. These long lace panels are particularly suited to bay windows or the very tall windows of high-ceilinged rooms.

OTHER TEXTILES

The latter part of the nineteenth century witnessed an increased **interest** in textiles, and it was the Arts and Crafts Movement in particular that elevated **textile craft** to a higher art form, improving the status of designers in this field. As a result, textiles of various forms are an **integral** part of the Arts and Crafts interior and can range from sophisticated **woven fabrics**, silk hand-embroidered **cushion covers** and table mats, to the revival of **American** textile techniques.

There are many **modern versions** of original Arts and Crafts pieces. **Ethnic** textiles and

Morris's Woodpecker Tapestry.
This is one of the very few tapestries designed entirely by Morris. The borders bear the legend, 'I once a king and chief, now am the tree-bark's thief, ever twist trunk and leaf, chasing the prey.'

HOW TO RECOGNISE ARTS AND CRAFTS WALL HANGINGS

Sunlight should not fall directly onto a wall hanging, as it will fade.

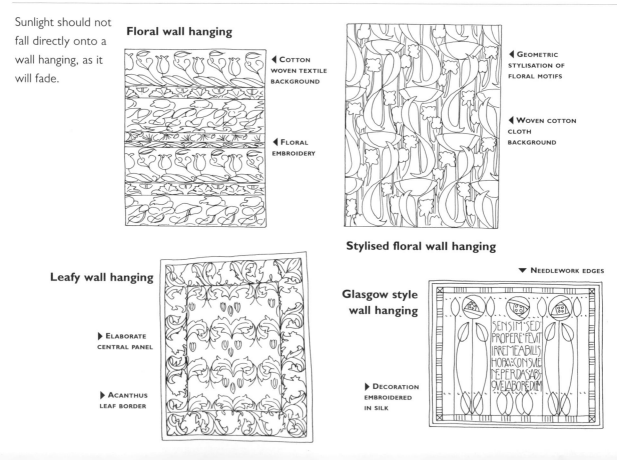

Floral wall hanging

◀ **COTTON WOVEN TEXTILE BACKGROUND**

◀ **FLORAL EMBROIDERY**

◀ **GEOMETRIC STYLISATION OF FLORAL MOTIFS**

◀ **WOVEN COTTON CLOTH BACKGROUND**

Stylised floral wall hanging

Leafy wall hanging

▶ **ELABORATE CENTRAL PANEL**

▶ **ACANTHUS LEAF BORDER**

▼ **NEEDLEWORK EDGES**

Glasgow style wall hanging

▶ **DECORATION EMBROIDERED IN SILK**

Wall hangings have a long history dating back to the tapestries and embroidered cloths traditionally hung in mediaeval halls. Morris, in particular, had a great enthusiasm for the use of fabric wall coverings and it is somewhat ironic that he, as a great designer of wallpaper, regarded the latter as second best to a hanging.

Embroidered panel (silk on linen), designed for Morris & Co. by J. H. Dearle, c.1885. Morris was particularly influential in reviving traditional methods of weaving and embroidery, and passed on much of his knowledge to his assistant and ultimate successor, J. H. Dearle.

Pomona designed by Edward Burne-Jones, c.1885. Although never a partner of Morris & Co., the painter Burne-Jones provided most of the firm's figurative designs for tapestry and stained glass. Morris designed the floral background and border design.

The linear design of this woven wool hanging is attributed to Ann Macbeth, the successor of Jessie Newberry as teacher of fabric design at the Glasgow School of Art, c.1905.

traditional style quilts look good hung on the walls or draped over a bed. **Quilts** provide a strong dose of **colour** and there's no reason why such a piece should not be applied as a wall hanging to **brighten up** plain white walls or wooden panelling. It's amazing how cushions, wall hangings and **linens** can immediately change the look and feel of a room.

An American quilt such as this one, made in 1888, would complement an Arts and Crafts interior.

OTHER TEXTILES

Whatever use they were put to – cushion covers, bed linen, runners or chair backs – embroidered, woven and printed textiles tended to feature floral motifs.

Printed silk designed for the Wiener Werkstätte, Lotte Froemmel-Fochler, 1912. Although the Wiener Werkstätte designers were influenced by the English Arts and Crafts Movement, they were also willing to embrace Modernism.

Silver Studio woven silk and cotton, double cloth, 1898. Silver Studio contributed directly to the reputation of British textiles on the Continent and when Liberty & Co. opened, it was Silver Studio textile designs that proved most popular.

Liberty & Co. woven silk panel designed by Arthur Willcock, c.1900. Although Willcock's textile designs display highly original and attractive patterns, his name is little known within the history of textile design.

Alexander Morton linen and chenille panel, c.1900. Like Morris, Morton experimented with natural dyes and fabrics. He founded his highly successful works in Ayrshire, Scotland, along the same principles as Morris & Co.

Alexander Morton double weave silk panel, c.1900. Morton contracted many of the leading Arts and Crafts designers of the day to do textile designs, notably Voysey and Butterfield.

This exquisite Tree of Life embroidered bedspread has a rustic feel traditional to the craft of American needlepoint. Its intricate pattern is best offset by plain walls and textiles.

Jessie Newberry table runner embroidered silk and wool with stylised flower motif. Newberry taught embroidery at the Glasgow School of Art and was influential in introducing the Glasgow style to textile design.

Morris's Apple Tree design embroidered silk on linen, c.1880. Morris and later Arts and Crafts textile designers advocated a much more creative approach to embroidery through a freer translation of designs and the use of natural dyes and fabrics.

Cushion cover with Morris's Trellis design by Beth Russell. Although Morris did not design Trellis to be worked as a cushion cover, it actually proves rather effective for this purpose because the square format of the trellis is in harmony with the square shape of the cushion.

A Glasgow School table runner of embroidered wool on linen with a geometric design attributed to Ann Macbeth. The linear nature of this design is characteristic of the Glasgow style.

LIVING ROOM

Designers in the Arts and Crafts Movement advocated a **bold** and **imaginative** use of **upholstery** fabric as a means of introducing points of **colour**.

Leather upholstery is a good option for Arts and Crafts furniture. It is timeless, comfortable and – if well-treated – lasts for years.

Furthermore, colours and **patterns** could be mixed up according to the size of the room and the number of pieces of **furniture** in question. In the case of this open-plan living-dining area, the exuberant and colourful **fabrics** add a decorative **focus** in an interior where there is a lot of exposed **brick** and **woodwork.**

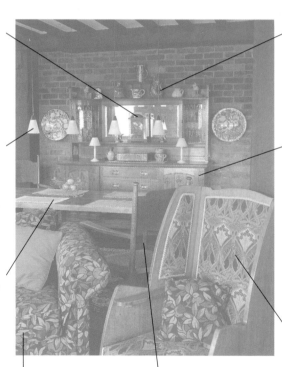

Oak mantel clock, c.1900, with arched top, exposed bell, brass dial with raised pattern and brass edging.
SEE PAGE 98

Simple modern reproduction lights hung in traditional 'Mackintosh style' as promoted by the Glasgow School of Art.
SEE PAGE 120

Refectory style table with central runner and X-braced legs.
SEE PAGE 76

Orangery fabric by Sanderson's enables the most modern of sofas to fit in with the rest of the room. Here, organic motifs of apples and leaves reflect Arts and Crafts imagery.
SEE PAGE 46

Oak carver armchairs by William Birch with solid curved backs and rush seats.
SEE PAGE 64

Ceramics collection from the late eighteenth, nineteenth and twentieth centuries, with plates, jugs and vases.
SEE PAGE 112

Oak sideboard, c.1895, by J. A. S. Schoolbred & Co. Includes mirror with curved stained glass cupboards at either side. The lower cupboard doors feature hand-carved motifs of vine leaves and grapes and brass handles.
SEE PAGE 86

Liberty-style oak hall chair with solid panel sides, upholstered in fabric designed by Charles Rennie Mackintosh.
SEE PAGE 64

UPHOLSTERY

Arts and Crafts style is marked by a simplicity in the treatment of upholstery fabric, and a total avoidance of frills and flounces. Armchairs and sofas in particular can accommodate a **strong design** both in terms of colour and repeats. Simple **Paisley** prints can work well, too, for the upholstery of armchairs or sofas. Alternatively, **geometric designs** can work if the overall interior is relatively plain. Geometric designs became **popular** during the first few years of the twentieth century due to the

Oak armchairs designed by Stanley Webb Davies. Davies's furniture is characterised by his passion for natural materials; he drew links between the furniture we make and the forest trees and animal hides that 'gave it birth'.

COVERING FURNITURE

Morris used his bold woven designs such as Peacock and Dragon and Briar Rose for the armchairs at Kelmscott Manor. Voysey's and Dearle's large fabric designs based on conventional natural forms also worked well for upholstery.

Plain cotton is ideal for upholstery fabric – especially if other fabrics in the room are highly patterned. A rich, earthy colour is ideal for much-used furniture.

Linen fabric has a wonderful texture and is easy to maintain. A neutral colour complements patterned wallpaper and curtains.

Morris's Jasmine design. Arts and Crafts designers advocated a non-uniform approach to upholstery. Different upholstery fabrics can be combined in one room so long as they suit the style of furniture.

Morris's Golden Lily design. Morris's fabric designs are particularly effective as upholstery fabrics, even if this was not originally his intended use. Their bold motifs can add an interesting focus to the plain, firm shape of a sofa or armchair.

Morris's Arbutus design. Originally designed for wallpaper, this pattern is also highly effective as a furnishing fabric because the hard lines of the pattern are softened when seen in folds.

The Drawing Room

at Standen, Sussex, was designed in 1890 by Philip Webb and furnished with Morris & Co. designs. The reclining chair on the left is upholstered in one of Morris's most popular designs for this purpose, Utrecht Velvet, while the other chair is upholstered in leather with a cushion in Morris's famous Trellis design.

A wing armchair in oak upholstered in Hera Peacock Feather fabric designed by Arthur Silver, c.1900. The Peacock Feather design was made famous by the commercial success of Liberty's from the end of the nineteenth century onwards and was applied to a number of mediums apart from upholstery fabric.

William Morris's ebonised chair upholstered in Bird woollen tapestry, c.1870. Bird was woven in wool as a double cloth and consists of alternating pairs of birds, with wings folded and spread, facing and turned away from each other.

Gustav Stickley drew direct inspiration for this design from Morris's reclining chair. However, unlike Morris, Stickley preferred to employ bold designs based on geometric, rather than natural forms, for upholstery fabrics.

influence of 'New Art' from the Continent and the impact of Charles Rennie Mackintosh and the Glasgow School of Art. Geometric designs can also work well to **embellish** Mission-style furniture and were favoured by the designer Gustav **Stickley**. **Leather** was the favoured choice of American designers Greene & Greene, Stickley and Frank Lloyd Wright. Its **smooth** texture provided a **subtle**

Liberty style. A Kentigern lounge armchair in oak with leather-upholstered sling back designed for Liberty & Co., c.1910.

contrast to their characteristic heavy use of natural woods. **Long plain cushions** can look particularly effective either as a window seat or on a wooden bench.

ALTERNATIVE MATERIALS

Leather, plain rich cotton, linen or woven fabric can work well as upholstery, especially if offset by carefully chosen cushions. The more worn the leather is – as long as it is well treated – the more beautiful it becomes.

Dark purple leather

Burgundy leather

Rust leather   **Brown leather**   **Dark green leather**

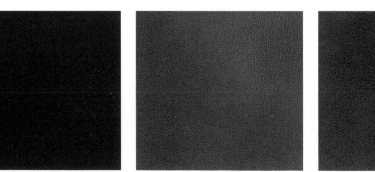

Although leather is a highly attractive medium for upholstery, it needs to be kept out of direct sunlight and high levels of light, since it is an organic material and is affected by extremes in temperature and humidity. A leather-upholstered armchair can therefore work well as a corner chair in a library or living room.

Two oak Arts and Crafts chairs from a dining set upholstered in white leather.

An oak wing chair with arm supports and leather upholstered seat and back designed by Ambrose Heal, c.1900.

A Liberty-style oak armchair with slatted sides upholstered in original burgundy leather. The design of this chair is attributed to Leonard Wyburd, who was the manager and designer of the store during its formative years.

Chapter 3

FURNITURE

Simple design and honest materials are hallmarks of Arts and Crafts furniture. A wide range including settles, chairs, desks, cabinets, beds, wardrobes and dressers was made to suit every home. Subsequent furniture designers have added their own distinctive touch.

LIVING ROOM

American Craftsman homes were based on the bedrock virtues of **beauty, simplicity, utility** and **organic harmony**. Furthermore, their interior designs relied on exposed structural elements, such as **wooden beams** and **stonework,** for decorative details. The latter are enhanced by charming accessories such as these **Stickley**-style reclining armchairs and settles upholstered in a mixture of different but **complementary fabrics**. The curtains are kept simple in keeping with the style of the room.

A Stickley-style armchair is made more comfortable with an upholstered cushion in a pretty eggshell blue.

The high-beamed ceiling, exposed fireplace, white walls and natural light give this room a spacious, barn-like feel.
SEE PAGE 18

The lattice-backed settle is reminiscent of those marketed in England by Liberty & Co. and Ambrose Heal.
SEE PAGE 72

The Dirk Van Erp lamp, copper tray and candleholders on the oak-topped side table are in keeping with the craft revival style.
SEE PAGE 104

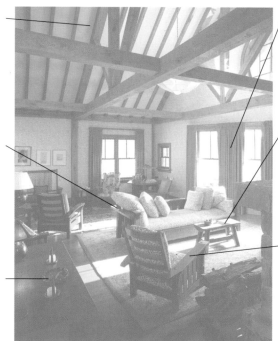

The overall colour tones of this room – red curtains, and pink and light green upholstery – are in perfect balance.
SEE PAGE 56

The roughly hewn coffee table has a farmhouse look which adds to the rural feel of this living room.
SEE PAGE 76

The Stickley reclining chairs are in geometric harmony with the ceiling rafters.
SEE PAGE 64

CHAIRS

The simple oak **ladder-back** Sussex chairs designed by Ford Madox Brown provided the prototype for Arts and Crafts dining chairs. Produced by Morris & Co. from 1866, they were relatively **inexpensive**. The most popular design featured a **hand-crafted** rush seat and legs connected by a plain stretcher. Gustav Stickley was instrumental in the introduction of Sussex chairs to the United States and his simple Mission dining chair was designed very much along the same lines. Today, **Sussex** and **Mission** chairs have become **sought-after** items. When choosing designs for dining chairs, look for **honest construction**, natural wooden materials, ladder-back or hard-back design, and **finely crafted** rush or leather seating. The Sussex chair was produced in a **variety** of styles: as a corner chair, **armchair**, settle and round chair, and many furniture designers of the Arts and

Oak chair for the Ingram Street Tea Rooms in Glasgow (Scotland) by Charles Rennie Mackintosh. A number of Mackintosh's chair designs, including this one, are manufactured today by the Italian firm Cassina, who work under a license from Glasgow University.

HOW TO RECOGNISE ARTS AND CRAFTS CHAIRS

Simple in design and construction, Arts and Crafts chairs are usually made from local hardwoods such as oak with rush or leather seating.

Sussex style

▶ SINGLE RACK OF DECORATIVE SPINDLES

▶ RUSH SEAT

Frank Lloyd Wright chair

▶ DISTINCTIVE VERTICAL SLATS

◀ LEATHER UPHOLSTERY

Glasgow School style

▶ MACKINTOSH-STYLE SQUARE MOTIFS

◀ EBONISED HIGH CHAIR BACK

Arts and Crafts architects, notably Frank Lloyd Wright and the Greene brothers, recommended their clients buy Stickley furniture if they weren't able to afford architect-designed originals. The Stickley Manufacturing Co. remains in production in New York State to this day.

A pair of oak rush-seated side chairs with heart cut-outs, designed by C. F. A. Voysey. As with many Arts and Crafts furniture designers, Voysey was an architect by training.

Mahogany chair by Ernest Gimson. The demand for light and movable chairs first catered for by Morris & Co. with their Sussex range meant that Gimson's chair-making workshop in Gloucestershire flourished until his death in 1919.

Chair designed by Voysey in 1898. Constructed from oak with a rush drop-in seat, this simple yet highly elegant chair was one of Voysey's favourite designs. He had several in the dining room of his own house in London.

Mackintosh Argyll chair designed in 1897 for Glasgow's Argyll Tea Rooms. This high backed oak chair, with its white calico upholstery and a stylised cut-out of a bird in flight in the chair-back, was Mackintosh's first chair design.

Crafts Movement created their own version. The famous Morris chair with its adjustable back, ebonised plain wood, and **cushioned seat** and back was the nineteenth-century equivalent to the recliner, designed specifically for its **beauty** and **comfort**. In homage to his English hero, Gustav Stickley made many versions of the Morris chair, although heavier in design and more **simply backed**. Mission chairs influenced other American furniture designers particularly those of the Grand Rapids, U.S.A. Chair designs with a **geometric emphasis** by Charles Rennie Mackintosh and the Austrian Wiener Werkstätte were emulated by G. Charles P. Limbert and Co. of Grand Rapids.

Solid oak chair with heart-shaped cut-out and rush seating, which reveals the consolidation of the work of many Arts and Crafts designers, notably C. F. A.Voysey, Ford Madox Brown and Ernest Gimson.

Ambrose Heal Letchworth rush-seated ladder-back armchairs in oak, c.1905. Heal's cottage furniture was designed for the Showcase Housing Exhibition at Letchworth, the first English garden city.

OTHER ARTS AND CRAFTS CHAIRS

Morris Sussex armchair

◄ SINGLE RACK OF DECORATED SPINDLES

► RUSH SEAT

Arts and Crafts designers adapted the Sussex and Mission style chair to suit different purposes.

Gordon Russell armchair

► SIMPLE JOINERY

◄ LEATHER LATTICE BACK & SEAT

Stickley armchair

► ADJUSTABLE BACK

◄ GRADUATED SLAT BACK

◄ CURVED SWELLED LEGS

► LEATHER UPHOLSTERY

► EXPOSED JOINERY

Ladder-back armchair

Original pieces of Morris furniture – particularly Sussex chairs – can still be found in their various forms. Tones of green are typical to an Arts and Crafts interior.

An armchair, probably designed by Ford Madox Brown after traditional chairs from Sussex. Very large numbers of these chairs were made and sold very cheaply.

Liberty & Co. satin-wood chair. Liberty's established their own furniture-making workshops in which they used the work of many British designers.

Oak armchair designed by Ernest Gimson in 1903, made in Peter Waals's workshop in 1923. Waals was a Dutch cabinetmaker who came to England in 1900 to work with Gimson, with whom he remained until Gimson's death in 1919.

Glasgow School oak barrel armchair with teardrop cut-out motif to inclined back slat, made by Wylie & Lochhead, c.1905. By the 1880s, Wylie & Lochhead employed over 1,700 people to create furniture taken from the designs of the Glasgow School of Art in Scotland.

Liberty & Co. Thebes stool, 1884. This stool was part of a popular set of furniture designed by Leonard Wyburd which incorporated stylistic influences from Egypt and North Africa.

A barrel chair in mahogany with upholstered seats and slats extending from arm to sledge base. Attributed to J. S. Henry, c.1900.

A rocking chair produced from a design by Gustav Stickley. The simple use of oak latticework and the unfussy, yet complementary, upholstered seat are all marks of American Arts and Crafts Mission furniture.

Oak armchair or Swan chair designed by C. F. A. Voysey in 1883–5. This is Voysey's earliest known furniture design and is often described as the Swan chair, although there is no evidence that Voysey gave it this title himself.

Liberty & Co. Wyclif rush-seated chairs in walnut. The strong geometric design of these chairs is attributed to Leonard Wyburd, the first manager of Liberty's.

J. & J. Kohn rocking chair in mahogany-stained beech designed by Gustav Siegel, c.1900. Although German designers were influenced by the English Arts and Crafts advocation of simplicity and fitness for purpose, they rarely executed their own designs, which were made for them by skilled craftsmen using modern machinery.

Extravagant throne chair in walnut with leather seat by G. Fisseux. This flamboyant chair with its imposing Gothic style falls into Morris's second category of furniture – State furniture.

Music armchair in oak with original studded leather seat designed by Richard Riemerschmid, c.1900. Riemerschmid was a highly daring German designer who wholeheartedly embraced the machine. His Maschinenmöbel (reasonably priced machine-made furniture) was enormously popular in Germany.

LIVING ROOM

There is a strong sense of **geometric harmony** in this living room, helped by the lines of the **Mission-style settles** and tables, and the **architectural glass** windows. The simplicity of these furnishings produced by

Gustav Stickley commands a unique sense of **gravitas** appropriate to a living room, which Stickley called 'the executive Chamber of the household where the **family** life centres'.

William Morris's Sussex settle was based on his original Sussex chair with rushed seat.

Stickley settles are still being made at his old workshop in New York State in the USA.

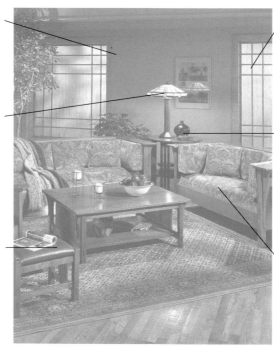

Pale olive green walls are a common feature of an Arts and Crafts interior.
SEE PAGE 18

The table lamp provides a soft glow and, with its wooden stand and geometric stained glass pattern, is the perfect finishing touch.
SEE PAGE 120

Leather was a popular upholstery material especially among American Arts and Crafts designers.
SEE PAGE 56

The architectural stained glass complements the strong geometry of the Stickley-style furniture.
SEE PAGE 118

Charming accessories such as ceramic vases strategically placed on side tables can help to give a room character.
SEE PAGE 112

The severity of this solid oak Stickley-style settle is offset by the floral pattern of the upholstery, and the soft rug.
SEE PAGE 72

SETTLES

Arts and Crafts designers recommended the **settle** because of its associations with a vanishing rustic past. Settles were a common feature in a **mediaeval interior** as a means of protection against draughts, the high back giving shelter to the sitter. A renovated church pew or a simple **wooden bench** lined with **cushions** give an Arts and Crafts look. Long wooden benches work well in a **hall** or around a large **oak kitchen table**. For a more comfortable approach, a simple modern sofa design can be carefully **upholstered** in keeping with the rest of the room. The **natural shape** of the sofa should be kept, and no trimmings added.

A hall seat in mahogany with high slatted back and blanket box base labelled Liberty & Co., c.1900. This would probably have been designed and marketed for a long hallway.

HOW TO RECOGNISE ARTS AND CRAFTS SETTLES

The most common settle designs feature a plain oak frame and back furnished with a long upholstered seat cushion.

Baillie Scott settle

▶ SOLID WOOD BACK STRETCHER

◀ WOODEN DECORATIVE INLAY

Roycroft settle

▶ LATTICE BACK

▲ PAINTED OAK

Settle with drawers

▶ WOVEN LINEN UPHOLSTERY

◀ PANELLED BACK

▶ OAK DRAWERS

The prototype of the futon sofa bed: an all-oak Stickley settle with a pullout bed beneath. Unstained oak and the simple pattern of the upholstery fabric provide a fine complement to the wood-panelled walls of this interior.

Mundus polished beech settle in the style of Joseph Hoffman. A Mundus black polished beech sofa upholstered in fabric designed by Hoffman. Hoffman – like Morris and other exponents of the Arts and Crafts movement – believed that the work of an artisan must be measured on the same level as that of a painter or sculptor.

William Morris's Sussex rush-seated settle was as popular as the Sussex chair thanks to its relatively low price and adaptability within an interior.

Oak settle by Sidney Barnsley, c.1919–23. Barnsley designed many versions of the settle with a chamfered lattice back.

LIVING ROOM

Arts and Crafts designers produced tables for **every room** in the house, not just the dining room. Although **occasional tables** are useful in a living room for the **effective** positioning of **table lamps**, metalwork and other decorative objects, they are only **appropriate** in an Arts and Crafts interior so long as they fulfil their **mission** of usefulness. A room should not be cluttered up with extraneous **tables**, especially if they are not **in keeping** with the rest of the interior.

Modern furniture designers such as Darrell Peart have been influenced by Arts and Crafts craftsmanship and style.

This stencilled border of floral motifs provides a neat demarcation between the wood panelled walls and the plain white-beamed ceiling.
SEE PAGE 32

Stickley based the design for his famous reclining chair on William Morris's prototype.
SEE PAGE 64

Wooden candlesticks enhance the American Craftsman feel of this room.
SEE PAGE 98

This Stickley-style cabinet provides an ideal means of storage for books as well as continuing the geometric theme of the interior.
SEE PAGE 86

Copper lamp bases, complete with a yellow-leaded glass shade, were particular to the American Arts and Crafts Movement.
SEE PAGE 120

Geometric patterns were made popular by Gustav Stickley and Greene & Greene, and are particularly suitable for a Stickley-style settle.
SEE PAGE 72

The pink-red tones of the large rug provide a warm focus in the largely wood-dominated interior.
SEE PAGE 36

TABLES
In the Victorian house, most tables would have been heavily covered in fabrics: the thought of leaving wood **exposed** was completely unacceptable. The message from Arts and Crafts designers was to have only table surfaces that fulfilled a **function**. A simply designed **pine** or **oak** table lacking in ornamental finery enhanced an interior and cut down on clutter. Arts and Crafts furniture designers reacted against the use of heavy mahogany and veneer and advocated **honestly constructed** trestle tables from **native** woods. Their large practical tables are reminiscent of those used in long **mediaeval dining halls**.

A fine dining table surrounded by simple dining chairs provided the **focal point** of a dining room – one of the most important rooms where a family gathered daily.

Mahogany table by Charles Rennie Mackintosh, 1918. The squares of mother-of-pearl inlay on the surface of this table impose a strong graphic element on what is essentially a simple table design.

HOW TO RECOGNISE ARTS AND CRAFTS TABLES

The Arts and Crafts table is characterised by a simple use of natural, unstained woods – mainly oak, pine and mahogany.

Gordon Russell table

◀ SCRUBBED PLAIN OAK SURFACE

◀ SOLID TIMBER TABLE SUPPORTS

Gimson table

▶ ENGLISH WALNUT WOOD

◀ TAPERED LEGS

Frank Lloyd Wright table

▶ SOLID OCTAGONAL SUPPORTS

◀ RECTILINEAR SLATS

Booth Howell table and four high-backed chairs in oak with metal and leather detail.

Mahogany table by W. R. Lethaby. The wavy line of the table legs set on golden bases gives this table a distinctly Gothic air.

Mission table designed by Stickley, whose furniture became known as the Mission style partly because of his frequently repeated statement that 'a chair, a table, a bookcase or bed [must] fill its mission of usefulness as well as it possibly can'.

Square oak table with ceramic ball feet by A. W. N. Pugin. Between 1844 and his death in 1852, Pugin designed over 1,000 pieces of furniture from the study of mediaeval originals, including 100 tables and 49 armchairs.

Pugin's side table was designed as a travelling table. It is made in solid oak and finished with oil and wax.

Oak side table designed for Morris & Co. by Philip Webb. Morris left Webb in charge of furniture production after Webb built and designed most of the interior for Morris's Red House in Kent.

Ambrose Heal & Co. dining table and six chairs in walnut, c.1922. The table has lattice end supports and ebony stringing, and the chairs have lattice backs and ebony dowels, a reflection of Gimson's and Barnsley's influence. Thanks to Heal's espousal of the machine, his furniture designs reached a wider proportion of the market than hand-crafted furniture.

Oak Mission dining table. By the beginning of the twentieth century, Mission-style furniture had become highly popular in the United States, to the point that retailers were scarcely able to keep up with the demand.

This Morris pine table is one of the few items of furniture designed by Morris himself and was made for the rooms he shared with the Pre-Raphaelite painter Burne-Jones in London during the mid-1850s.

Due to its integral role in family life, the dining room must be considered as one of the most important rooms in the house. This impressive Stickley table with the imposing Harvey Ellis chairs provide a ceremonious atmosphere in this dining area.

Table attributed to J. D. Crace, one of Pugin's main collaborators. This octagonal table was possibly a copy of a Pugin design that was originally exhibited at the Mediaeval Court at the Great Exhibition, London in 1851.

Elaborate oak 'Side Table' designed by Bruce J. Talbert, whose furniture is characterised by the use of unstained oak and rich, elaborate mouldings based on naturalistic designs.

Contemporary designers are still influenced by the Arts and Crafts style. American designer Darrell Peart was recently inspired by a 1909 Greene & Greene dining table to make this piece.

HOME OFFICE

Arts and Crafts **desks** were built in all shapes and sizes – such as flat-topped, drop-leaf and rolltop – but all were a perfect marriage of **form and function**. Women's desks were often placed in the main **bedroom**, which doubled up as a sitting room where the lady of the house would retire at certain times of the day to write her **letters** and maybe even a **journal**. Other desks were often located in the **library** – usually the husband's domain. These days, as the line separating the roles of rooms has blurred, desks tend to be found in the **living room** or **home office**.

This walnut writing table with leather top, c.1870, makes an elegant desk for a home office.

Oak dresser with copper strap hinges and mirror is a beautiful and light storage facility. It is also useful for displaying ornaments such as a copper planter with floral motifs.
SEE PAGE 90

Pewter ornaments such as a Liberty's Tudric biscuit barrel, a Warwick clock, a candlestick and a box styled after Archibald Knox, unite the elements in the room.
SEE PAGE 104

An oak occasional table with stylised tulip motifs provides a useful surface for a candle or lamp, a picture frame and a book.
SEE PAGE 76

Oak reclining seat upholstered in Morris's Acanthus and Bird fabric design.
SEE PAGE 64

A pair of rush-seated beech Sussex side chairs provide extra seating in case of visitors.
SEE PAGE 64

White walls are the perfect backdrop for a room busy with furniture and fabrics. The green-painted dado rail is in keeping with Arts and Crafts interiors.
SEE PAGE 18

Oak bureau with stylised tulip piercings and drop-leaf front. Once the desk is opened, correspondence can be stored in pigeon-holes, and the flat leaf is an ideal writing surface. Books can be stored on the shelves below.
SEE PAGE 82

A mahogany flat-topped desk with pigeonholes for storing letters. The flat top enables work to be spread over an area, thereby providing a more roomy option.
SEE PAGE 82

DESKS

DESKS The earliest supporters of the Arts and Crafts Movement tended to be **intellectual** and **artistic**, so the desk was an important **feature** of the home. The American designer Charles Rohlfs produced numerous desk designs from about 1900 onward constructed from **oak** with **carved** decorations. Like other Arts and Crafts furniture these are now out of reach of most people's budgets, but there are many alternative **desk** designs on the market. A simple wood design with a flat **leather** top is a good choice, as is a desk with **pigeonholes** to store paperwork.

An English walnut writing table made around 1870. Arts and Crafts furniture makers, such as Gimson and Barnsley, were responsible for a revival in walnut, a timber that had fallen out of favour in the early eighteenth century because of the popularity of mahogany.

HOW TO RECOGNISE ARTS AND CRAFTS DESKS

Natural materials, clean lines and clever storage make an Arts and Crafts desk a timeless, yet practical choice.

Stickley flat-top desk

◀ EXPOSED DOVE-TAIL JOINTS

◀ EXPOSED BRASS FITTINGS

Gothic 'State' style desk

▶ NEO-GOTHIC PINNACLES

▶ GOTHIC CARVING

Writing desk with pigeonholes

▶ LEATHER MAT SET INTO WRITING FLAP

▶ JAPANESE OAK

This modern-day Stickley oak desk and storage unit fulfil a highly practical function, but because of their aesthetic beauty they don't appear too utilitarian.

The lightness yet solidity of this modern desk designed by American furniture-maker Darrell Peart points to Greene & Greene's influence.

Desk for Hill House bedroom in Helensburgh near Glasgow by Charles Rennie Mackintosh, c.1904 (both open and closed). Mackintosh's desks and cabinets tend to be highly decorative with various inlays of mother-of-pearl and coloured glass. The interior of this desk is fitted with pigeonholes and a practical, sliding writing surface.

This highly decorative bookcase and desk by R. Norman Shaw combines the grandeur of Morris's State furniture and Pugin's decorative interpretation of Gothic motifs and forms.

Marquetry escritoire and stand, designed by George Jack for Morris & Co., 1893. In 1890 George Jack became chief designer to Morris & Co., and was responsible for many of the quasi-eighteenth-century pieces carried out in mahogany with inlaid decoration.

An oak writing desk designed by Voysey illustrates how solid oak and elaborate metal hinges can give a writing desk a distinct mediaeval feel equal to that of Voysey's Kelmscott Cabinet (see page 88).

Roycroft writing desk (both open and closed). The Roycroft community was a commercial enterprise and artists' colony founded by Elbert Hubbard in East Aurora, New York State. Roycroft furniture is characterised by its extreme simplicity and was perhaps the most mediaeval in appearance of American Arts and Crafts furniture.

Desk by Harvey Ellis.
Ellis briefly joined Stickley's workshop in 1903, where he was influential in adding a touch of grace to the firm's furniture production.

The Jugendstil style was named after *Jugend*, the innovative periodical published in Munich which disseminated new ideas of design based on the Art Nouveau love of sinuous curves and individual craftsmanship.

CABINETS

William Morris acknowledged two categories of furniture: necessary **everyday** furniture, such as chairs and tables; and **State** furniture – cabinets and sideboards 'which we have quite as much for beauty's sake as for use'. The State cabinets produced by Morris & Co. were **highly decorated** and painted with mediaeval

This St George oak cabinet – designed by Philip Webb with painted panels by Burne-Jones – was an attempt to construct the Romantic chests and cabinets depicted in Pre-Raphaelite painting.

designs. However, these furniture pieces were very **expensive** and generally commission-based. Later designers such as Voysey and the craftsmen community in the Cotswolds produced **simple, plain wooden** cabinet designs, often with the hinges and metalwork exposed as a **decorative** feature. Liberty's established their own cabinet-making workshops, which produced simple **country-style** oak dressers. Similarly, American furniture designers favoured the solid wooden style as opposed to the ornate painted cabinets first produced by Morris & Co.

How to Recognise Arts and Crafts Cabinets

Cabinets of this period range from the highly ornate example of the late Gothic revival to the simple plain oak designs of American Mission furniture.

Drop fronted cabinet

▶ DROP WRITING FRONT

Cabinet with inlaid wood

◀ INLAID WOODEN FLORAL DETAIL

Oak sideboard

▼ OAK BACK

◀ HAND-PAINTED ART NOUVEAU STYLE MOTIFS

▲ WALNUT WOOD HANDLES

▲ SUBTLE CURVED FRONT

Marquetry cabinet in walnut, ebony and holly with whitebeam drawers and silver fittings, designed by Ernest Gimson, 1906. For this design, it is thought that Gimson was inspired by Spanish *bargueño* cabinets and spice cabinets with small drawers typical in the seventeenth century.

Hugh McKay Baillie-Scott display cabinet in oak with chequer and pewter inlay, c.1900. Baillie-Scott's numerous furniture designs, over 140 in total, were sold through Liberty's and John White's showrooms in London.

Cabinet with painted decoration by Charles Rennie Mackintosh. This display cabinet was designed in 1902 as part of a pair for Mackintosh's own use in his Main Street flat in Glasgow. The interior of the cupboard doors is adorned with stylised female figures proffering large rosebuds.

A glazed mahogany cabinet inlaid with brass, ebony and box-wood, with brass fittings, c.1904. Sinuous curves were the hallmark of Joseph Hoffman's furniture designs for the Secessionist School based in Vienna.

The sideboard or buffet server was a favourite among Gustav Stickley and his circle, and contained many storage compartments as well as a useful display space within a dining or living room. The handwrought metal handles and hinges give this oak Mission-style piece an appropriately rustic feel, particularly if used to display Arts and Crafts pewter or ceramics.

The Kelmscott Cabinet, designed by Charles Voysey, c.1899. This idiosyncratic oak cabinet was commissioned by Morris to house the original copy of his Kelmscott Chaucer published in 1896. The simplicity of the design and wood is set against highly decorative lettering and floral brass fittings.

Wall cabinet with elaborate incised ornament designed by John Moyr Smith and manufactured by Cox & Sons. The latter started out as suppliers of ecclesiastical furniture, later branching out as cabinet carvers and manufacturers of artistic furniture.

Walnut sideboard with plate stand designed by Ernest Gimson, made by Ernest Smith and Percy Burchett in 1915. Gimson's workshop was very labour-intensive. The plate rack of this sideboard took 453 hours to construct and the metal handles took 98 hours.

Oak sideboard probably designed by George Freeth Roper. Similar to the work of Godwin's later 'cottage' furniture, Roper was accused by Godwin of 'slavish imitation'.

Satinwood cabinet with painted panels, c.1877, designed by E. W. Godwin. Godwin was an early collector of Japanese prints and crafts, which may have influenced the painted panels and delicate wooden struts of this cabinet. His later, simpler, furniture designs were known as 'cottage' furniture.

New Studio sideboard in oak with three cupboards and one drawer below leaded-glass doors, all with brass handles, produced for Liberty & Co., c.1898.

KITCHEN DRESSERS
Before the introduction of modern kitchen units, the **dresser** was a stock feature of most kitchens. It provided useful storage space and a means of displaying **decorative tableware** and **ceramics**. Whether it includes a suitably rustic pine dresser or cabinet or not, the Arts and Crafts kitchen is **simply designed** with a lot of exposed **natural** woodwork, **shelving** and **racks**. Functional equipment should be kept clear of the surface area as much as possible.

Pine kitchen dresser, mid-nineteenth century. Today, well-made pine dressers are often available in less exclusive antique shops.

How to Recognise Arts and Crafts Dressers

Conceal labour-saving kitchen equipment with wooden cabinets and dressers to create a kitchen based on the Arts and Crafts style.

Heal & Son dresser

▶ **Oak lattice back**

Gimson dresser

◀ **Solid pine shelving**

Gothic style

▶ **Solid mahogany back**

▲ **Simple oak catch**

◀ **Carved ornamental detail**

▲ **Exposed pine panels**

'**We believe** in having the kitchen small, so that extra steps may be avoided, and fitted with every kind of convenience and comfort, with plenty of shelves and cupboards.' (Stickley, 1909).

Hanging Mission wall rack constructed from solid oak, a wall rack is a useful means of displaying prized ceramics and reducing clutter on surfaces.

Stained oak dresser by Ernest Gimson, 1902–5. Initially made for his large country kitchen, Gimson and Barnsley designed many different versions in oak and other less expensive woods.

Oak dresser by W. R. Lethaby, c.1900. The bold dark and light inlays of this dresser are typical of Lethaby's later furniture designs. This design was adapted and popularised by Ambrose Heal.

BEDROOM

Prior to the Arts and Crafts Movement, **bedrooms** were **furnished** and decorated in a similar manner to the drawing or living room, with numerous pieces of furniture and as little **light** as possible. Within the Arts and Crafts home, however, the bedroom was regarded as a **sanctuary** of natural **simplicity** with a light decorative scheme and essential furniture only. This solid **Stickley-style bed** and chest of drawers are skilfully crafted from oak, and they are offset by plain white walls and **minimal** decoration.

This oak wardrobe by Barnsley looks deceptively simple, but the skill involved in the curve of the front was immense.

For the first time, plain white walls became completely acceptable within an interior.
SEE PAGE 18

The cushions scattered across the bed are upholstered in Morris's Acanthus design, produced in a red pattern.
SEE PAGE 52

The bedlinen produced from Morris's fabric designs provides a decorative focus among the plain woodwork and white walls.
SEE PAGE 52

Simple metal accessories, such as the bedside lamp on the side table, and the pot and vase on the chest of drawers, add to the rustic feel of this bedroom.
SEE PAGE 120

Morris's Wandle design works well as a fabric for curtains.
SEE PAGE 46

Suites of wooden bedroom furniture were popular with Arts and Crafts designers. This bedroom features a wooden bed frame with a complementary chest of drawers and bedside cabinet.
SEE PAGE 94

Soft rugs on the bedroom floor soften the coldest stone, tile or wooden flooring. Sisal rugs and rush matting were also popular at the time.
SEE PAGE 36

BEDROOM FURNITURE

On the whole, Arts and Crafts bedrooms were furnished simply and designed as **havens** of uncluttered tranquillity. William Morris advised low-key decorative schemes for bedrooms, with simple wooden furniture, plain walls and lots of **natural light**. American and British craftsmen produced a range of beds constructed from solid wood but today it is often more practical to adapt wooden or brass bedsteads to a contemporary **bed frame**. A simply designed wooden wardrobe and chest of drawers finish the room. **Willow wicker** furnishings can offer a suitably light feel to a bedroom and are a less expensive option than heavy wooden pieces. And **white-painted** furniture can have a soothing effect. Anything that is not essential should be avoided.

Harvey Ellis night stand.
Constructed from solid oak with handwrought copper handles for the two small drawers. Ellis's designs tend to be lighter and more delicate than his colleague Stickley's.

HOW TO RECOGNISE ARTS AND CRAFTS BEDROOM FURNITURE

Ambrose Heal dressing table

◀ TOILETTE MIRROR

▶ GENEROUS DRAWERS

▶ EXPOSED DECORATIVE BRASS HANDLES

Peter Waals wardrobe

▶ GEOMETRIC FACETED FRONT

▶ STURDY SUPPORT

◀ INLAID DECORATION

Peter Waals dressing table

Bedroom furniture was restricted to a bare minimum. Furniture designs and colours were always complementary.

▼ CARVED DECORATIVE BANNER

◀ SOLID OAK FRAME

Gordon Russell bed ends

This beautiful Arts and Crafts oak wardrobe is inlaid with heart-shaped Ruskin enamels, stylised lily fruitwood panels and features cruciform ring handles.

Oak wardrobe from the Moreton bedroom suite retailed by Liberty & Co. The simple geometric nature of this design works well in a small bedroom or dressing room.

An eccentric chestnut wood wardrobe designed by Ambrose Heal around 1904. The owl design is a throwback to the idiosyncratic use of animal forms of earlier Arts and Crafts designers, notably William de Morgan and Walter Crane.

Athelstan bedroom suite designed for Liberty & Co. around 1909, comprising a washstand with dark-green inset tiles and a chest of drawers and mirror – all with heart cut-out motifs,

An ambitious oak wardrobe from Barnsley's Gloucestershire workshops. The curved design of the wardrobe front is unusual and must have involved considerable skill.

The Prioress's Tale wardrobe was designed by Philip Webb in 1859 for William Morris's Red House in Kent. It was painted with a Chaucerian theme by the Pre-Raphaelite painter Edward Burne-Jones.

Glasgow School oak wardrobe with inlaid panels of floral motifs in various woods by Wylie & Lochhead, c.1905. By 1905, the furniture produced by Wylie & Lochhead had become a household name throughout Scotland and England.

Three-door wardrobe with Glasgow rose motifs inlaid in copper, abalone and various woods. Design attributed to George Logan and made by Wylie & Lochhead, c.1900. Like Charles Rennie Mackintosh, an inlaid copper rose motif was the hallmark of Logan's furniture designs.

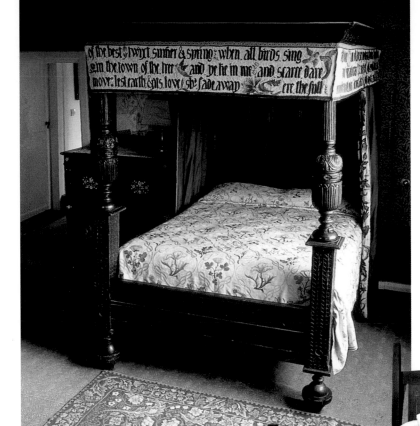

In Morris's bedroom at Kelmscott Manor, Gloucestershire, the valance – embroidered by Jane and May Morris – illustrates a poem by Morris which celebrates the natural beauty of the Gloucestershire countryside he loved.

This Harvey Ellis style Mission bed with inlay is still available from the Stickley workshops in New York State.

Stickley bedpost and panel bed with leather. This post and panel bed is based on a Gustav Stickley design, although it is now larger and taller than the original. The headboard panels are also available in solid wood.

MISCELLANY

Although the **Arts and Crafts** Movement decried the cluttered appearance of Victorian interiors, there is no doubt that the addition of miscellaneous pieces such as an **imposing** grandfather clock, sleek umbrella **stand**, discreet magazine rack or handcrafted wooden **coffer** can beautify a room and add an idiosyncratic touch. Collectors can search in antique stores and contact suppliers for unusual objects that will give them great **pleasure** and also provide a talking point for their guests. These objects are **practical** too, which means that their homes won't be overrun by useless knick-knacks.

Glasgow School umbrella stand in oak with cut-out handhold to the back and brass uprights. Designed by George Walton, c.1900.

Mission-style tall case clock.

HOW TO RECOGNISE ARTS AND CRAFTS DESIGNS

Common motifs include cut-out hearts and the use of natural materials such as wood and copper.

Box with inlaid wood

▶ EBONY INLAY

◀ WALNUT WOOD

Umbrella stand

▼ SECTIONS OF CHAMFERED WOOD PANELS

▲ WROUGHT STEEL DRIP TRAY

▼ OAK FRAME

◀ MESH-LIKE LATTICED FRONT

Radiator cover

▼ EMBROIDERED SILK PANELS

▶ OAK FRAME

Screen

An imposing entry is one of the characteristic spaces of the Arts and Crafts house. The impressive nature of this hallway is enhanced by the magnificent gong and the beautiful yet simple wooden and copper umbrella stand.

Roycroft magazine/book pedestal.

Oak coffer with bronze strapwork hinges extending from top to full length of back. Retailed at Liberty's, the coffer was made by Mrs Alfred Waterhouse's Yattendon Metalworking Class (created to give occupation to the men in her village in the evening). The class disbanded in 1914 at the outbreak of World War One.

Glasgow School magazine rack in mahogany with round cut-outs to the back and boxwood string-ing, c.1905.

Valkyrie upright grand piano in oak with pewter- and ebony-inlaid stylised flower motif, and steel strap hinges and feet. Designed by L. and F. Wyburd and made by J. J. Hopkinson for Liberty & Co., c.1902.

Chapter 4

ORNAMENTS Numerous small

workshops were set up in America and Europe to

create the metalware, ceramics and glassware that

are such a joy to collect today. As well as providing

job satisfaction for workers, workshops kept craft

skills alive in the face of booming mass production.

HOME OFFICE
Hand-forged Arts and Crafts metalware was used as hardware in houses and on furniture, particularly simple **copper** and **pewter** that featured **hammer dents**. Copper accessories by Dirk Van Erp are an attractive and practical addition to this **fireplace** in a New York State farmhouse. The fireplace was often the **centre** of attention in a living or drawing room – especially in winter – and the metalware, original pine **woodwork** and exposed **brickwork** make this one particularly welcoming.

Wrought-steel candelabra designed by Ernest Gimson, c.1905.

The Stickley lanterns with heart cut-outs complement the metal plate, box and vase on the mantel.
SEE PAGE 120

A drop-leaf writing desk was an important feature of the Arts and Crafts home and provided an aesthetically pleasing workspace.
SEE PAGE 82

A warming oven to the left of the fireplace is covered by a cast-iron plate.
SEE PAGE 104

The handwrought copper fireplace accessories by Dirk Van Erp include a screen, iron and fireplace tools.
SEE PAGE 104

Plain walls, exposed timbers and brickwork provide a perfect backdrop for this charming, American Craftsman-style home office.
SEE PAGE 18

A leather-upholstered Stickley armchair and footstool provide a comfortable corner in which to relax.
SEE PAGE 56

Wooden flooring was a common feature of an Arts and Crafts home. Here, the floorboards have been covered by a drugget rug like the ones that Stickley imported from India.
SEE PAGE 36

METALWARE

Arts and Crafts metalware, distinguished by the marks of the hammer and subsequent **rustic** appearance, was first made popular in England by the metalworkers of C. R. Ashbee's Guild of Handicraft. **Simply designed** metalware soon became an essential component of the Arts and Crafts interior, largely due to the commercial **success** of retailers such as Liberty's and to the low cost and **workability** of metal. Metalware was also highly popular in America, where Stickley and Roycroft both had extensive metalworking operations.

A picture frame in pewter with repoussé-work owl and stylised flower motifs. Thought to have been designed by Frank Bazeley, c.1904.

HOW TO RECOGNISE ARTS AND CRAFTS METALWARE

Many designers created a wide range of metalwork that incorporated decorative motifs such as animals and foliage.

Teapot
- ◀ BRASS HANDLE & FEET
- ▶ BEATEN COPPER

Plate
- ◀ PICTORIAL EMPHASIS
- ▶ EMBOSSED SILVER DECORATION

Coffee pot
- ◀ GREEN GLASS TOP
- ▶ PLAIN SILVER

Dish and cover
- ▼ LOOPED WIRE HANDLE
- ▶ ELEGANT LINES

Pitcher
- ▶ REPOUSSÉ DECORATION
- ◀ HAMMERED SILVER

Vase
- ◀ NATURALISTIC SILVER RELIEF
- ▲ RECTILINEAR VASE FORM

Like most original Arts and Crafts metalware, Heintz art metal vases are now collectors' items. Simple vase designs worked in bronze with an Arts and Crafts silver overlay floral design are the hallmarks of the Heintz style.

Mackintosh clock designed around 1900. Today, interest in Charles Rennie Mackintosh's fittings and fixtures is considerable and many of his designs are in current production.

Liberty Heritage Pewter
A design from the famous Tudric collection designed by Archibald Knox in 1902. The hallmarks of Liberty Tudric designs were the decorative Celtic forms and floral motifs which were widely admired and imitated.

Candlestick designed by Philip Webb for Burne-Jones, 1861. Webb appreciated both grandeur and simplicity in his metalware. He made the distinction between daily objects, which should be strong but not overly ornamented, and objects for beauty's sake alone.

Silver and enamel biscuit box designed by Archibald Knox in 1901. Highly practical, yet decorative, with Celtic floral motifs, mother-of-pearl and enamel insets.

Silver, brass and copper jug by Louis Comfort Tiffany, New York, c.1900. Although Tiffany is best known for his opalescent glassware, his designs were also adapted to other materials.

Pair of wrought-steel candelabra designed by Ernest Gimson, c.1905. As well as architecture and furniture, Gimson produced designs for leadwork, embroidery and pierced and chased metalwork.

Silver trinket box adorned with Celtic motifs in green enamel, designed by Archibald Knox in 1905 for Liberty's popular Cymric range.

Electroplated two-handled bowl with hinged cover by Christopher Dresser. His sparse tableware designs created from sheet metal inspired the Wiener Werkstätte and pointed to the later Industrial Aesthetic movement

A carved gilt-framed mirror designed by Dagobert Peche with a Wiener Werkstätte paper label, exhibited in the Austrian pavilion at the Paris Exhibition of 1925.

Chased and pierced brass wall sconce designed by Ernest Gimson, c.1905. Gimson set up his own smithy in Gloucestershire, where he produced numerous articles of metalware – such as door furniture and light fittings – in brass, polished steel and iron.

The hand-hammered appearance of this pewter clock case by Liberty & Co. has a rustic look, which foreshadows Knox's later Tudric designs.

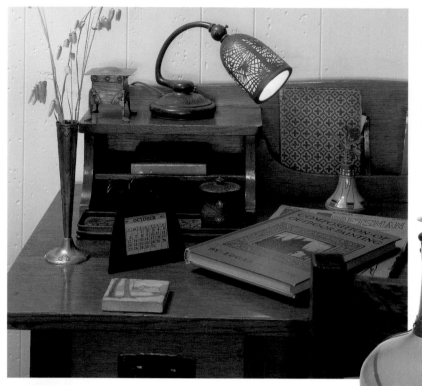

Metalware accessories like this lamp, vase and box add character and style to a writing desk, together with some books from the Arts and Crafts era.

A Liberty Tudric pewter owl jug with inset seashell eyes taken from a design by C. H. Brannam, c.1902. Although Tudric pewter was almost entirely machine-made, at first glance it has the appearance of being handwrought.

Silver-mounted green glass decanter with maker's mark for the Guild of Handicraft, 1901. This guild, founded by Charles Robert Ashbee, first made handbeaten or hammered metalware popular, but the project did not survive because of Ashbee's antipathy to machine production and commerce.

Liberty & Co. rose bowl with Celtic strapwork decoration, 1908. Liberty launched its Cymric silver range alongside Tudric pewter. Although it was largely machine-made, it was finished with 'a touch of honest hammering'.

Pair of candlesticks by R. L. Llewellyn Rathbone, 1902. Features beaten copper with bands of punched floral ornament. Rathbone had a wide knowledge of metalworking techniques, which he taught at Liverpool University and the London Technical Institute.

Brass teapot by Voysey, 1896. The simplicity of this teapot harks back to the Middle Ages. Although Voysey trained as an architect, no aspect of an interior – from fire-tongs to kettle – was too small to win his attention.

Liberty copper repoussé oval mirror, c.1905, features large inset turquoise Ruskin enamel ornaments. The **rectangular mirror**, c.1900, has stylised flower motifs and two inset Ruskin enamel ornaments. **Wall sconces**, c.1900, have a fish and shell motif. Liberty's competitive prices enabled professional firms' designs to reach a wide public – even providing a name, *stile Liberty*, as an alternative to the style more generally known as Art Nouveau.

DINING ROOM

The Victorian **dining table** was an ornate affair, with elaborate linens, crockery and cutlery. The Arts and Crafts Movement advocated a **simpler approach** based around a number of beautifully designed accessories such as this **Rockwood dinnerware**. The **buffet server** became a typical feature of an Arts and Crafts dining room, as it not only fulfilled a **practical** function – providing a surface from which to serve food – but it was also a means of **displaying** ceramics and metalware.

Glass goblet designed by James Powell, c.1905. Arts and Crafts glassware and ceramics were less elaborate than their Victorian counterparts, and their beauty came from the skilful crafting of the material itself.

The buffet server was an integral feature of the Arts and Crafts dining area and proved an effective way to display ceramics and metalware.
SEE PAGE 86

Simple table mats and runners on an undressed table are more typical of an Arts and Crafts dining room than fine, delicate white linens or silks.
SEE PAGE 50

A studded band – often known as the Shreve Strap – distinguishes Shreve & Company's Gothic-inspired silverware cutlery.
SEE PAGE 104

Mica shades with copper hardware were favoured by Arts and Crafts designers for lamps, because they offered an indirect and soft light, creating a tranquil ambience.
SEE PAGE 120

Lustre glaze ceramic ware was popularised by designers of the Arts and Crafts Movement.
SEE PAGE 112

Rockwood dinnerware provided a simple alternative to the overly ornate ceramics of the Victorian era.
SEE PAGE 112

CERAMICS & GLASS

Art pottery became a phenomenal **success** in Britain largely due to the work of William de Morgan, who produced a wide range of ceramics decorated with **floral** forms. He was also inspired by **Islamic** designs. Other British potteries of renown were the Martin Brothers, Della Robbia and Moorcroft. As with de Morgan, their motifs were principally floral and leafy with exceptional **lustre glazes**. These potteries were aided by the enormous **commercial** success of Liberty's as a retailer through

Tall-necked vase decorated in the Persian manner, 1912; **high-shouldered vase** decorated with panels of dog rose, 1903; both by Richard Joyce.

Galleon vase with heraldic devices by William S. Mycock, 1914. The Pilkington Tile and Pottery Co. was primarily a glassworks until 1897, after which they also produced Royal Lancastrian lustre-ware.

HOW TO RECOGNISE ARTS AND CRAFTS CERAMICS

Art pottery with Islamic influences and lustre glazes are characteristic of the period. Common ceramics motifs include flowers, leaves and animals.

William Grueby vase

◄ CONICAL VASE FORM

◄ GEOMETRIC FLORAL MOTIF

William de Morgan plate

◄ HIGHLY PICTORIAL DECORATION

William de Morgan plate

◄ LUSTRE DECORATION

▲ FLORAL AND FAUNA MOTIFS

Newcomb vase

► WHITE FLOWERS IN RELIEF

◄ SIMPLE VASE FORM

Liberty & Co. bowl with lid

◄ ELABORATE EMBOSSED LID

► RICHLY COLOURED GLAZE

Arts and Crafts matte glazed pottery was admired for its restrained use of natural motifs and earthy colours.

A painted and glazed vase with flower motif by P. Revere, Boston (USA), c.1910.

Water jugs in the form of a comical pelican, heron and owl by Brannan. The decorative use of animal forms was a characteristic of the Arts and Crafts designers.

The Upchurch Potters sold their wares through Liberty & Co. This pottery is characterised by a minimum amount of surface decoration and strong shapes. Colours were mostly monochrome and the designs were inspired by Roman prototypes.

William de Morgan plate. De Morgan 'rediscovered' the lost art of lustre decoration for pottery. Although he is now best known for his tiles, he produced ceramic tableware which is characterised by its boldness of design and strong use of colours.

A 25-piece tea set by Foley Peacock Pottery with stylised Glasgow rose motif, comprising six cups, saucers and biscuit plates, a sandwich plate, milk jug, cream jug, sugar bowl and cover, and slops dish, designed by George Logan in 1903.

Goblet designed by James Powell, c.1905. Powell's of Whitefriars, London, was one of the most prestigious glassworks of the nineteenth century. They provided coloured glass for the production of stained glass by Morris & Co.

Tiffany cameo vases Tiffany located his glass factory in Corona, Queens (USA) in 1893. Thanks to the success of his glassware, he soon had over 300 workers, designers, artists and glass-blowers at the works.

Loetz gold glass vase c.1900 covered with multicoloured iridescence and applied purple spot and stripe decoration, also a Loetz purple iridescent **bowl** to the Austrian Secessionist Kolomon Moser.

which they sold their wares. Art pottery became enormously **popular** in America with the foundation of such companies as the Chelsea Keramic Art Works at Boston, which developed a number of **sumptuous glazes.** The Rockwood Pottery and ceramicist William Grueby perfected a variety of colours and wares which became widely accessible.

Louis Comfort Tiffany dominated the production of **decorative** glass in America and developed a number of glassmaking techniques, inspired by his own expertise and knowledge of **Roman** and **Middle Eastern** glass, such as **millefiori** and lustre. In 1893, he registered his Favrile (meaning **handmade**) trade-

Charger decorated with a ship by the Della Robbia Pottery, Birkenhead. Their art pottery, made in emulation of Italian prototypes, proved enormously influential largely thanks to the fact that it was stocked by Liberty & Co.

Blue and gold Favrile 'Jack in the Pulpit' glass vase, 1915, by Louis Comfort Tiffany (USA).

mark, which went on sale three years later with enormous commercial success. Although Tiffany also produced ceramics, it is his **iridescent** glass vases and lamps that are now his main legacy.

HOW TO RECOGNISE ARTS AND CRAFTS GLASS

Decorative, iridescent and coloured glass in bold shapes are hallmarks of Arts and Crafts style.

Glass decanter

▶ SILVER TOP

◀ DECORATIVE LEAD SWIRLS

Wine glasses

▶ CONICAL STEMS

▲ SOLID HEAVY BASE

Glass vase

◀ BUBBLY EFFECT OF CLUTHRA GLASS

▶ OPAQUE BASE

DINING ROOM

American Arts and Crafts architect and designer Frank Lloyd Wright adopted a **geometric** approach to stained glass design, which was **integral** to his architecture at the time. In this dining room at Willits House, built in 1902 in Illinois, there is a strong sense of **harmony** based on the skilful interplay between the **horizontal** and **vertical** lines of the windows, furniture and the **structure** of the room itself, which gives it a formal, ceremonial feel.

Flora and fauna motifs were also popular for stained glass, and modern designs have carried on the tradition.

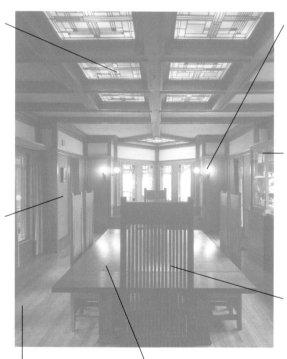

Geometric stained glass in the ceiling and windows of this dining room allow light to fall in golden pools on the floor and table. Frank Lloyd Wright was revolutionary in choosing a geometric pattern for his stained glass.
SEE PAGE 118

Dark green painted walls add a classic touch to the room, relieved by the wooden panelling fitted on the walls. White paint has been used above the window and dado rail, which lightens the whole atmosphere.
SEE PAGE 19

Wall lamps spread a subtle light over the room. The need for overhead lighting is stunningly fulfilled by the stained glass windows in the ceiling.
SEE PAGE 120

A built-in cabinet suits the clean lines of the room and, with its own special lighting, is a perfect display case for prized ornaments, ceramics and metalware.
SEE PAGE 86

Frank Lloyd Wright oak dining chair, c.1903, designed to complement the scheme of the Willits House dining room. When used around the dining table, these high-backed chairs create the effect of a room within a room.
SEE PAGE 64

Wooden flooring provides the finishing touch to a room that is grand, yet warm and airy.
SEE PAGE 36

Frank Lloyd Wright oak dining table, c.1903, designed as part of a set with oak high-backed chairs.
SEE PAGE 76

STAINED GLASS

The revival during the nineteenth century of the **mediaeval art** of stained glass was partly caused by a spate of ecclesiastical building. Morris & Co. was instrumental in introducing stained glass into the home, using clear glass with **painted detail** in paler tones. Through the pioneering work of designers such as Henry Holiday and Christopher Wall, stained glass was used not only in **windows**, but also inset into **doors** and **furniture**. Stained glass was also extremely popular in America. Louis Comfort Tiffany and John La Farge employed layers of **translucent** glass adorned with **rich designs** of flowers, exotic birds and stylised motifs. Later designers such as Charles Rennie Mackintosh and Frank Lloyd Wright used coloured glass, generally unpainted, to create **geometric designs** as part of their decorative schemes.

An ornamental stained glass window with floral motif shows that, sometimes, less is more.

HOW TO RECOGNISE ARTS AND CRAFTS STAINED GLASS

Flora and fauna and geometric designs feature heavily in Arts and Crafts stained glass.

Hallway window

▶ FLORAL MOTIFS

◀ GEOMETRIC BACKGROUND

▶ ARCHITECTURAL STAINED GLASS

Geometric style

Flora and fauna

▶ HIGHLY ORDERED FLORA AND FAUNA

▶ GEOMETRIC LEADED BACKGROUND

◀ TREE OF LIFE WINDOW

Waterlilies and fish

▶ FLUID LINES

◀ FLORA AND FISH MOTIFS

Peacock image

▶ IRIDESCENT GLASS

▲ NATURALISTIC PEACOCK

◀ ABSTRACT PATTERN WORK

◀ BOLD USE OF LEAD

Abstract design

Briar Rose A modern design using common Arts and Crafts motifs of flora and fauna.

'Spring' illustration for Morris's *The Earthly Paradise* by Charles E. Kempe. By the end of the nineteenth century painted glass had become a regular domestic feature. This design was for Wightwick Manor in Staffordshire.

Modern stained glass designers can produce beautiful results that reflect the Arts and Crafts style, as shown in this bakery window with its harvesting theme.

Dorigen roundel designed by Edward Burne-Jones and set in a background of floral quarried tiles designed by Morris and Co., c.1876. Morris & Co. gained their initial commercial success through the revival of mediaeval stained-glass techniques. Whereas Burne-Jones provided most of the designs, Morris was concerned with technique and colour.

LIGHTING

The invention of the **light bulb** by Edison in 1879 opened up new possibilities for designers as it allowed them to dispense with oil reservoirs, gas pipes and the hazards of naked flames. W. A. S. Benson designed numerous lamps, including **glazed pottery** ones inset with **glass**, and **copper** chandeliers. In America, **natural forms** such as flowers inspired lamp design, as the stems could disguise wires and the petals hide light bulbs. Tiffany lamps **glowed** romantically in dark corners, and Stickley and the Roycroft shops produced plain **wooden** lamps in keeping with the Craftsman style.

Suspended light designed by Frank Lloyd Wright for Dana-Thomas House, Illinois (USA) in 1902. It's thought that Lloyd Wright was inspired by butterfly wings.

Tiffany's leaded-glass lampshades can add a romantic warmth to dark corners of a room, because – unlike spotlights – they diffuse the light in a uniform manner.

HOW TO RECOGNISE ARTS AND CRAFTS LAMPS

Lighting should be subtle and bring out a room's colour scheme. Corner and table lamps are preferable to a strong overhead light.

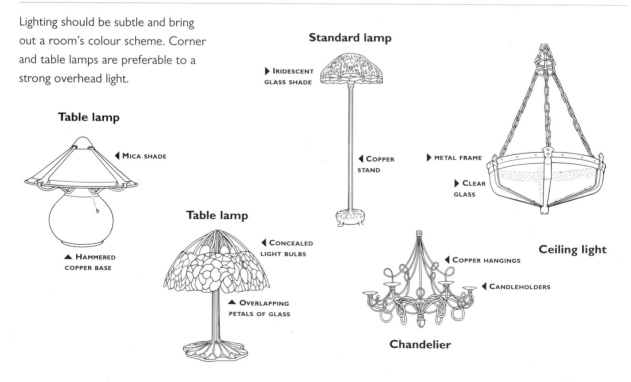

Standard lamp
- ▶ IRIDESCENT GLASS SHADE
- ◀ COPPER STAND

Table lamp
- ◀ MICA SHADE
- ▲ HAMMERED COPPER BASE

Table lamp
- ◀ CONCEALED LIGHT BULBS
- ▲ OVERLAPPING PETALS OF GLASS

Ceiling light
- ▶ METAL FRAME
- ▶ CLEAR GLASS

Chandelier
- ◀ COPPER HANGINGS
- ◀ CANDLEHOLDERS

The yellow mica shade of this standard lamp offers a glowing light appropriate to the intimacy of the Arts and Crafts interior.

Table lamp inspired by the clean lines and simple design of American Arts and Crafts designers. Arroyo products are finished by hand, so no two look exactly alike.

Tiffany Studios 10-light lily pad table lamp with assorted iridescent glass shades, c.1900. Natural forms, especially flowers, were used by Tiffany to disguise the functional elements of lighting. In this case, the stems hide the wiring and the drooping petals conceal the lightbulbs.

Arroyo Craftsman takes inspiration from the art glass of Frank Lloyd Wright and the natural materials used by Stickley and Greene & Greene. This ceiling light features gold and white iridescent glass and an antique copper finish.

A pair of copper and enamel electric light brackets designed by Charles Robert Ashbee, c.1895. Ashbee's beaten or hammered metalwork was a very popular material for lighting as it provided an interesting surface from which the light could be deflected within a room.

SUPPLIERS

Antiques

Arts and Crafts Movement Art
Furniture
158 Camden Street
London NW1 9PA, UK
T: +44 (0)20 7267 4324
F: +44 (0)20 7267 5199
www.artfurniture.co.uk

Decorative Arts
27 Gloucester Road
North Laines
Brighton
Sussex BN1 4AQ, UK
T: +44 (0)1273 676 486

H. Blairman & Sons Ltd
119 Mount Street
London W1Y 5HB, UK
T: +44 (0)20 7793 0444

Hill House Antiques and Decorative
Arts
PO Box 17320
London SW3 2WR, UK
T: +44 (0)7973 842 777

Liberty plc
Regent Street
London W1R 6AH, UK
T: +44 (0)20 7734 1234
F: +44 (0)20 7573 9876
www.liberty-of-london.com

Mallett
141 New Bond Street
London W1Y 0BS, UK
T: +44 (0)20 7499 7411
F: +44 (0)20 7495 3179

Paul Reeves
32b Kensington Church Street
London W8 4HA, UK
T: +44 (0)20 7937 1594
F: +44 (0)20 7938 2163

The Millinery Works Ltd
85/87 Southgate Road
London N1 3JS, UK
T: +44 (0)20 7359 2019
F: +44 (0)20 7359 5792

Stickley
Stickley Drive
PO Box 480, Manlius
NY 13104-0480, USA
T: +1 (315) 682-5500
F: +1 (315) 682-6306
www.stickley.com

The Arts And Crafts Home
28 Gloucester Road
North Laines, Brighton
Sussex BN1 4AQ, UK
T: +44 (0)1273 600073
www.arts-and-crafts-home.fsnet.co.uk

Reproduction and modern

Ceramics and glass

Liberty plc.
Regent Street
London W1R 6AH, UK
T: +44 (0)20 7734 1234
F: +44 (0)20 7573 9876
www.liberty-of-london.com

Fireplaces

Amazing Grates Ltd
61-63 High Rd
East Finchley
London N2 8AB, UK
T: +44 (0)20 8883 9590
F: +44 (0)20 8365 2053

Furniture

Darrell Peart
177 Western Avenue West
Seattle, WA 98119, USA
T: +1 (425) 277-407
F: +1 (425) 988-017
www.furnituremaker.com

Liberty plc
Regent Street
London W1R 6AH, UK
T: +44 (0)20 7734 1234
F: +44 (0)20 7573 9876
www.liberty-of-london.com

A. Sanderson & Sons Ltd
Sanderson Road, Uxbridge
Middlesex UB8 1DH, UK
T: +44 (0)1895 238244

Liberty plc
Regent Street
London W1R 6A, UK
T: +44 (0)20 7734 1234
F: +44 (0)20 7573 9876
www.liberty-of-london.com

Stickley
Stickley Drive
PO Box 480, Manlius
NY 13104-0480, USA
T: +1 (315) 682-5500
F: +1 (315) 682-6306
www.stickley.com

Leather

Bill Amberg
The Workshops
31 Elkstone Road
London W10 5NT, UK
T: +44 (020) 8960 2000
F: +44 (020) 8960 2321

Lighting

Arroyo Craftsman
4509 Little John Street
Baldwin Park
California 91706, USA
T: +1 (626) 960-9411
F: +1 (626) 960-9521

David Jones
65-77 Market Street
Sydney, NSW 2000
Australia
T: +61 (02) 9266 5544
F: +61 (02) 9267 4770
www.davidjones.com.au

Lead & Light
35A Hartland Road
London NW1 8DB, UK
T: +44 (0)20 7485 0997
F: +44 (0)20 7284 2660

Liberty plc
Regent Street
London W1R 6AH, UK
T: +44 (0)20 7734 1234
F: +44 (0)20 7573 9876
www.liberty-of-london.com

Paint

Fired Earth
Twyford Mill
Oxford Road
Adderbury
Oxon OX17 3HP, UK
T: +44 (0)1295 812088
F: +44 (0)1295 810832
www.firedearth.com

Murobond Superior Paints
81-83 Dickson Avenue
Artarmon, NSW 2064
Australia
T: +61 (02) 9906 7299
F: +61 (02) 9439 7593
www.murobond.com.au

Rugs

J. R. Burrows & Company
PO Box 522
393 Union Street
Rockland, MA 02370, USA
T: +1 (781) 982-1812
F: +1 (781) 982-1636
www.burrows.com

David Jones
65-77 Market Street
Sydney, NSW 2000
Australia
T: +61 (02) 9266 5544
F: +61 (02) 9267 4770
www.davidjones.com.au

Liberty plc
Regent Street
London W1R 6AH, UK
T: +44 (0)20 7734 1234
F: +44 (0)20 7573 9876
www.liberty-of-london.com

Beth Russell
Designer's Forum
PO Box 565
London SW1V 3PU, UK
T: +44 (0)20 7798 8151
F: +44 (0)20 7233 8118

Stencils

Stencil Library
Stocksfield Hall
Stocksfield
Northumberland NE43 7TN
UK
T: +44 (0)1661 844844
F: +44 (0)1661 843984

Textiles and wallpapers

J.R. Burrows & Company
PO Box 522
Rockland, MA 02370, USA
T: +1 (781) 982-1812
F: +1 (781) 982-1636
www.burrows.com

David Jones
65-77 Market Street
Sydney, NSW 2000
Australia
T: +61 (02) 9266 5544
F: +61 (02) 9267 4770
www.davidjones.com.au

A. Sanderson & Sons Ltd
Sanderson Road
Uxbridge
Middlesex UB8 1DH, UK
T: +44 (0)1895 238244
F: +44 (0)1895 830045

Liberty plc
Regent Street
London W1R 6AH, UK
T: +44 (0)20 7734 1234
F: +44 (0)20 7573 9876
www.liberty-of-london.com

Beth Russell
Designer's Forum
PO Box 565
London SW1V 3PU, UK
T: +44 (0)20 7798 8151
F: +44 (0)20 7233 8118
www.bethrussellneedlepoint.com

Fired Earth
Twyford Mill
Oxford Road
Adderbury
Oxon OX17 3HP, UK
T: +44 (0)1295 812088
F: +44 (0)1295 810832
www.firedearth.com

Tiles

Kenneth Clark Ceramics Ltd
The North Wing
Southover Grange
Southover Road
Lewes
East Sussex BN7 1TP, UK
T: +44 (0)1273 476761
F: +44 (0)1273 479565
www.kennethclarkceramics.co.uk

Fired Earth
Twyford Mill
Oxford Road
Adderbury
Oxon OX17 3H, UK
T: +44 (0)1295 812088
F: +44 (0)1295 810832

Liberty plc
Regent Street
London W1R 6A, UK
T: +44 (0)20 7734 1234
F: +44 (0)20 7573 9876
www.liberty-of-london.com

Timber

Timber Floors Pty Ltd
7 Jumal Place
Smithfield
Sydney, NSW
Australia
T: +61 (02) 9756 4242
F: +61 (02) 9756 4242
www.timberfloors.com.au

HOUSES TO VISIT

Many of these houses have public tours, but it is wise to contact them in advance, just in case they have set times for viewing.

UK

Kelmscott Manor (William Morris)
Kelmscott
Nr Lechlade
Gloucestershire GL7 3HJ
T: +44 (0)1367 252486

Rodmarton Manor (Ernest Barnsley)
Cirencester
Gloucestershire GL7 6PF
T: +44 (0)1285 841253

Wightwick Manor (Edward Ould with Morris & Co. interiors)
Wightwick Bank
Nr Wolverhampton
West Midlands WV6 8EE
T: +44 (0)1902 761108

Great Maytham Hall (Sir Edwin Lutyens)
Rolvenden Cranbrook
Kent TN17 4NE
T: +44 (0)1580 241346

Standen (Philip Webb)
Nr East Grinstead
Sussex RH19 4NE
T: +44 (0)1342 323029

Blackwell (M. H. Baillie Scott)
Bowness-on-Windermere
Cumbria LA23 3JR
T: +44 (0)1539 722464

The Hill House (Charles Rennie and Margaret Mackintosh)
Upper Colquhoun Street
Helensburgh
Argyll and Bute E84 9AJ
T: +44 (0)1436 673900

Greywalls (Sir Edwin Lutyens)
Muirfield
Gullane
East Lothian EH31 2EF
T: +44 (0)1620 842144

Melsetter (W. R. Lethaby)
Island of Hoy
Orkney KW16 3M2
T: +44 (0)1856 791352

USA

Gamble House (Greene & Greene)
4 Westmoreland Place
Pasadena, CA 91103
T: +1 (626) 585-2171

Mission Inn
3649 Mission Inn Avenue
Riverside, CA 92501
T: +1 (909) 781-8241

Ennis Browne House (Frank Lloyd Wright)
2655 Glendower Avenue
Los Angeles, CA 90027
T: +1 (213) 660-0607

Hollyhock House (Frank Lloyd Wright)
Barnesdale Art Park
4809 Hollywood Boulevard
Los Angeles, CA 90027
T: +1 (213) 662-7272

Craftsman Farms (Gustav Stickley)
2352 Route 10 West
Manor Lane
Parsippany-Troy Hills, NJ 07950
T: +1 (973) 540-1165

Frank Lloyd Wright Home and Studio
951 Chicago Avenue
Oak Park, IL 60302
T: +1 (708) 848-1976

Oak Park Visitors Center (Frank Lloyd Wright)
Oak Park, IL 60301
T: +1 (708) 848-1500

Roycroft Community
Main and South Grove Streets
East Aurora, NY 14052
T: +1 (716) 655-0571

Stickley Museum
300 Orchard Street
Fayetteville, NY 13104
T: +1 (315) 682-5500

Grove Park Inn
290 Macon Avenue
Asheville, NC 28804
T: +1 (828) 252-2711

INDEX

Numbers in *italics* refer to captions

CREDITS

Quarto would like to thank and acknowledge the following for
supplying pictures and items reproduced in this book:

(Key: l left, r right, c center, t top, b bottom)

Amazing Grates: p41b; *Arroyo Craftsman:* p121cl/bl; *Beth Russell at
Designer's Forum:* p12bl, p36tr, p39br, p53c, p97t; *H. Blairman & Sons
Ltd:* p69br, p79 cl/cr, p88b, p89cr; *The Bridgeman Art Library:* p8, p21,
p22-23 all swatches, p24 tr/cl/ bl; p26tr; p31t, p33t,p38 all pics;
p39t&bl; p46cc, p50tr, p51br, p52tr/cc/cr, p57br, p64tr, p65cl/br,
p66tl, p67cl/cc/cr, p68tr/cc, p73cr/b, p76tr, p77cl/cr, p78tl/br,
p83cr/b, p84 all pics, p85b, p86tr, p87tl/bl, p88l, p89t/cl, p90tr,
p91r/b, p96tl/tr, p104tl/tr/bl, p105tr/bl, p108c/br, p109tl/tr,
p112tl/tr, p113cl, p115tr/cl, p119tl/c, p120tl, p121cr; *J.R.Burrows&
Company:* p24 cc/bc/cl/bl, p25 cr/br; p27c/b, p49 all pics; *Darrell
Peart:* p79b, p83cl; *Elizabeth Whiting & Associates:* p29, p35; *Fired
Earth:* p41t, p53tl; *Geoff Diner:* p10; *Kenneth Clark Ceramics:* p12cl,
p40 all pics; *Lead and Light:* p119tr/bl; *Liberty:* p103br, p113cr; *Mallett:*
p46, p82, p114cr; *The Arts and Crafts Home/Mark Golding:* p37b,
p65bl, p78tr, p103bl; *The Millinery Works Ltd/Jefferson Smith:* p51bl,
p53l/b, p56tr, p57cl, p65cl, p66tr, p67br, p69tl/tr/bl, p72tr, p73cl,
p77t, p78c, p87tr/br, p89b, p95l/r/b, p96bl/r, p98tl, p99cl/cr/b,
p104tr, p105tl/cr, p108bl/br, p109c/b, p114t/b; *Oakbrook Esser
Studios:* p120tr; *Paul Reeves:* p46cr, p51cl, p52bl/cc/br, p53tr, p106br,
p107br, p121br, p121br; *Paul Rocheleau:* p9, p117; *Pictor International
Ltd:* p37c; *Rob Gray:* p6, p27t, p63, p73t, p91t, p99tl, p103, p108t,
p111, p113, p121t; *Sanderson:* p19t, p23t, p25cc/bc/cr/br; p26 all
swatches; p37t, p45, p46bl/bc/br, p47t/cc/cr/bl/bc/br, p51t; *The
Stencil Library:* p32-33 all stencils; *Stickley:* p11bl, p57bl, p68b, p71,
p72, p77b, p78bl, p79t, p83t, p85tl/tr/c, p88t, p91c, p93, p94tr,
p97bl/br, p98tr, p99tr

Many thanks to the following people for allowing us to photograph
their homes: *Moira and Nick*, p2, p25t p31b; p57; *Sally and Ian*, p10bl,
p16, p66t, p80.